Dad ROCKS!

A COLLECTION Of POETRY

EDITED BY GEMMA HEARN

 Young**Writers**

First published in Great Britain in 2005 by
Young Writers, Remus House, Coltsfoot Drive
Peterborough PE2 9JX
Telephone: 01733 890066
Website: www.youngwriters.co.uk

Foreword

The book you are about to read is a heartfelt and youthful tribute to fatherhood. A competition was held to coincide with Father's Day, to give children and teenagers who enjoy poetry the opportunity to not only have their work published, but also to show how they feel for their dads. Be they thankful, emotional or humorous, these poems are sure to warm any heart, father or not, and are certain to be a welcome addition to your family bookshelf.

CONTENTS

Glenthorne High School, Sutton

Greensteds School, Kenya

Leys Farm Junior School, Scunthorpe

Meadowburn Primary School, Bishopbriggs

Oriel Bank School, Stockport

Ridgewood High School, Stourbridge

St Constantine's International School, Tanzania

THE POEMS

No Stranger

The whispers of a morning chill,
Shudder through the air,
A vision of a lonesome child,
Whom no one gives a care,
Lies amongst the debris,
Of a bitter life so cold,
The remains of once a happy dream,
Are battered, worn and old.

But suddenly some hope appears,
A candle in the night,
This hero needs no shiny shield,
Or vicious sword, to fight.
He takes my hand and leads me home,
Who is this man I see?
A rescuer he truly is,
A man who resembles me.

Daniella McLenaghan (14)

Winner!

Congratulations
Daniella!
From our selection of
prizes you chose to give
your dad a replica
Manchester United
football shirt for
Father's Day.

Dad in A million

I love my dad very much,
More than words can say.
He's always with me in my thoughts,
I love him more each day.
If I could choose who my dad was,
I wouldn't change a thing.
Because of all the dads in the world,
I think he is the king.
Camping trips and other treats
And holidays galore,
I'm happy that he is my dad,
I couldn't ask for more.
I think about him every day
And I know it's true,
That every day, no matter what,
Dad, I'll always love you!

Hannah Price (11)

Top
10

My Dad!

I call him a name,
A very special name,
A name that I call no one else.

Here's why ...

He makes me feel safe,
When no one else can,
That's why I call him that name.

He makes me laugh,
When I really want to cry,
That's why I call him that name.

I love him very much,
And he loves me,
That's why I call him that name.

The name I call him is Dad,
And he deserves that name in every way.

Helen Matheson (11)

my Dad's famous ...

My dad's a boxer,
The best I have seen,
He's tough and he's hard,
He's strong and he's lean.
My dad's a singer,
He's hit number 1,
He's won 'Pop Idol'
Five times, in a run.
My dad's a racer,
In the Grand Prix
He lifted the cup,
In 2003.
My dad's a dancer
In big West End shows,
He also does ballet,
He's got dancing toes.
My dad's an artist,
He paints all the time,
He could be famous,
But chose to be mine.

Emma Jacobs (12)

SOMEthing SPEcial

I close my eyes and take a deep breath,
I never meant what I just said.
I am ashamed and I dare not look up to see,
The look of horror that looks back at me.

But instead you just smile, pat me gently then walk away,
Telling me I should be more careful about what I say.
Dumbstruck, I mumble an apology.
Thinking, *how can he forgive me so easily?*
But you are my father and you understand me.
Therefore, you know what I say I don't always mean,
No matter how real it may seem.

But you are something special and sacred to me,
A priceless gift from wherever it may be.
So I am writing this poem to tell you,
That no matter what I say or do,
I will always love you.

Chorin Kawa (15)

My Dad

Top
10

To have a dad just like you,
Is to have a guardian angel all my life through,
To love and protect me, I admire and respect,
I just hope I live up to what you expect.

I just want you to know,
You mean the world to me,
Only a heart as pure as yours,
Would give so unselfishly.

The things you've done,
Every time you're there,
Gives me knowledge inside,
To see how much you really care.

Friends I can choose,
Relatives I'm stuck with,
But as my relative, my friend,
I'm glad, I love you no end.

Even though I may not say,
I am grateful for all you do,
I am blessed in having such a fun-loving dad,
A dad, my dad, that's you!

Joanne Healey (16)

untitled

The day I was born, you first loved me,
Holding me in your arms, a tiny little girl was all you could see.
Protecting me from the big world, too little to understand,
You guided me through life, and always held my hand.
Now I'm a big girl, I can face the world alone,
Falling in love, and one day leaving home.
But you'll always be my father,
Now and forever after.

Rebecca Wright

A POEM For Dad

I was only a lad when it happened,
You were ill and there was nothing you could do.
A tumour, they said, a benign one at that,
Why did it have to be you?

A new job for me, I was the man of the house,
What a hard job it was going to be.
Cuddling Mummy whenever she felt sad,
Sometimes she had to cuddle me.

You beat the tumour and that was fine,
We were relieved and glad to have you back.
Until disaster struck, you fell ill again,
This time a heart attack.

'What did I do to deserve this?'
I kept saying over in my head.
I was sad, lonely, depressed and angry,
To see you lying in that bed.

The years went by, we stuck together,
Through the good times and through the bad.
Sometimes I think I missed out on things,
Although sometimes I'm glad I have.

You give me hope and encouragement,
To be what I want to be.
You give me inspiration,
It means so much to me.

So Dad let me say, I'm glad you're my dad,
Your qualities are second to none.
I would like to say from the bottom of my heart,
I'm proud to be called your son.

Ryan Gibb (18)

Top 10

untitled

Fishing, sailing, motor mad,
Makes me laugh, then makes me sad;
Backs up Mum when I've done wrong,
Aren't I just the lucky one!

Presents scattered round the tree,
From me to Dad, from Dad to me;
Gratitude flowing through the air,
Smiles and laughter everywhere.

Special memories mean so much,
And Dad's just got that special touch,
To soothe me down when I feel distressed,
To tell me how to look my best.

Traipsing round a hundred zoos,
Waiting in the theme park queues;
Sharing hobbies, swapping jokes,
Eating home-grown artichokes.

Thank you for the love you've shown,
You'll never leave me on my own;
So Dad, although we'll move apart,
You'll be forever in my heart.

Victoria Brooks (14)

untitled

My dad is a punk rocker
with a flash red guitar,
his eyes as blue as skies,
his hair as black as tar.

My dad is a famous footballer,
best friends with famous Dave.
He has played against Wayne Rooney
and every ball shot, he saves.

My dad's a famous jockey
he beat Dettori at Ascot.
Dad's horse is called Lightning,
he is the fastest England's got.

My dad is a fireman,
he rescued me from the flames.
He has been knighted by the Queen
for rescuing damsels and dames.

So, maybe my dad isn't all that,
he isn't famous you see
but the reason my dad is the best,
is because he loves me.

Fleur Wheatley (12)

My Dad

My dad is so special,
He mucks around,
Always making a sound,
He is mad,
And never sad,
Does he make me laugh?
You bet he does,
He has twinkles in his eyes,
Even when he cries,
Can he cook?
He makes a mean beans on toast,
My dad sings wherever he goes,
He even does it for a living,
Would you love this dad?
I certainly do
I love you Dad.

Grace Reinhold-Gittins (10)

MY Dad

My dad is like a superhero
Protecting me and keeping me safe.
When I am on my Rollerblades
My dad is like a pillow to catch me if I fall.
My dad is like a clown.
He cheers me up when I am upset.
My dad is one of a kind
And I love him loads because he is special.

Bianca Moore (9)

MY Dad

My dad is brilliant, he is great,
He is my very best mate,
He is tall,
And is crazy about football.

My dad helps me with my English and maths,
And often takes me to the swimming baths,
My dad is a great help for my running,
He gives me plans, which are very cunning.

I guess after all you've heard, it's easy to tell,
That I love my dad more than the world itself,
That is why I would like to say: -
Have a very happy Father's Day!

Julie Dobbin (11)

My Dad

I'm always saying life's not fair
But as a kid I'm unaware
Of the great things my dad has done.

When I fell out of a tree
When I fell over and hurt my knee
My dad was there for me.

When I won a sports medal
When he took off my stabilisers I just had pedals
My dad was there for me.

When I finished primary school
The fancy dress parties, dressed like a fool
My dad was there for me.

I love my dad he's always there
He can be crazy with what he wears
But my dad is here for me.

Hannah Wright (12)

MY Dad

M akes me happy
Y ear in, year out

D oesn't argue and doesn't shout
A s each day goes passing by
D oesn't even make me cry

I nstead there's joy and happiness
S ince he is here with me

T o my dad a message is sent
H ow I love you
E ach day I do

B ecause you care
E very day and in every way
S o you just have to be ...
T he best dad in the world.

Daniel Whitehouse (11)

Father's Day

F abulous time
A ll about dad
T ons of laughter
H ave lots of fun
E njoying the day
R elaxing
S leeping

D oing absolutely nothing
A day of happiness
Y es, that's Father's Day.

Siobhan Fox (10)

ᴍY brilliant Dad

My brilliant dad
Spoils me rotten!
He is tall like a giraffe
He is a busy man
His skin is rough but I don't mind,
We like buying things and
Keeping them secret but sometimes
He gives away the secret and shouts out:
'Doh'

My brilliant dad
Happy when I'm happy
Cross when I've been naughty
Sad when I'm sad
My brilliant dad
Spoils me rotten.

Rebecca Mackay (8)

My Dad

My dad is cool,
My dad is bright,
My dad knows how to fix a light,
My dad's hard-working
He never stops, he reminds me of a bottle of pop
My dad's a great dad
I love him so much
And I wish I had two of him to kiss and cuddle.

Lauren Taylor (8)

Funky Father

F antastic, fab and funky and my fave foodmaker.
A mazing and agile.
T erribly untrendy.
H ouse king.
E verything I ever wanted
R idiculously lovable.

Imogen Nicol (12)

My Dad

He's great in many respects
Comedian, musician, intellect.

Champion ditherer, keeping the music industry afloat
He knows Bob Dylan's tunes note for note.

He's all of these things and a doctor on call
But he's also my dad, the most important of all.

Robbie Hunter (13)

My Dad

My dad is huge, especially to me,
I'm only a child,
I find him a giant because he's six foot three,
That's massive compared to me!

My dad is funny,
And can never resist a joke,
He's also good at rugby,
After all, he was my coach for three years.

My dad is interesting,
Full of amazing things,
Like how to properly kick with your shin,
Or how to use an axe properly.

My dad, I'm glad,
Is my favourite dad,
My only dad,
And nobody else's.

Ruairidh Nelson (13)

My Dad

My dad has always been there for me
When I needed someone most of all
My dad has always made me laugh when I am sad.

If I was having trouble in school my dad would help me out
My dad is the best there is no doubt.

My dad is nice, my dad is fun
My dad loves me, I love my dad
He has always said that he will be my friend
When there is no one there.

When my dad gets older I will take care of him.
Like he takes care of me.

Ryan Plusch (15)

My Dad

My dad likes beer
But still stays clear
He comes home late
In a bit of a state
I wouldn't want him to change
Because he is top of the range.

Ravinder Gill (9)

My Dad

My dad is brave,
My dad is clever,
He looks out for me,
And is always there,
We have fun together,
Playing and laughing,
My dad is really the best.

Shona Cordner (12)

untitled

My dad is super cool
But rubbish at pool.

He has got dark black hair,
And a belly like a bear.

He's got blue eyes like mine,
And when I'm hurt,
He always makes me feel fine.

He supports Man U and,
He's supported them since he was two.

For a man, he is quite small,
But he's proud of me for being good at football.

I love my dad to bits,
And I think the world is lucky to have him.

Garry Longshaw (12)

FaB Dad

Why don't you put your feet up,
And take the day off too,
Cos it must be very hard,
To be a dad as fab as you.

Rachael Low (10)

MY DADDY

Since my first grazed knee
Or the first bee that stung me
You were always there.

You held on tight
When I rode my first bike
And still you were there.

Even now I'm a teen
And I try to act dead mean
Even then you're there.

But now you're gone
The week seems really long
I'll see you soon and daddy
I love you!

Lucy Salisbury (14)

caring No 1 Dad

Dad, Dad, Dad is the best,
He cares for me and all the rest.
Dad, Dad, Dad is so kind,
So he and my mum get on
Well combined
Dad, Dad, Dad is so fun,
He takes me round the lake, to do a run
Dad, Dad, Dad is so special,
So special that he only suits
Me and my family.

Jessica Tonks (11)

MY EVERLASTING UNCLE

He calls me chicken legs and teases my brother,
He's sometimes silly and terribly funny.
He encourages me to try things that I have never done before.
He's precious to me for all the things we do together.
He's my special everlasting uncle.

Tabitha Gordon-Smith (8)

How i Admire my Father

How I admire my father
My interest of him will never tire
I admire him so much
Because he organises things as fast as a dart
Oh yes he is very smart

How I admire my father
He is always so tired
Because he works all day and night
For his family he must

How I admire my father
He cares for me so much
Even though he goes away
He still keeps in touch.

Jean-Marc McGhee (12)

My Dad

My dad is great
He buys me everything I want
I love him because he is so special and precious
I'm still his little princess
I love you Dad
I wish you were here.

Terri Lowe (11)

Dad

Strong yet gentle,
Fit but fair
You are a cuddly bear
You warm up my heart
When you smile.

Samantha Walton (11)

untitled

My dad is great
He's my best mate,
Always there,
Always strong,
Just one fault,
He's never wrong.

Gemma Jordan (11)

Dad!

My dad's the greatest,
He's the best,
He has hairs,
Upon his chest.

He loves football,
He loves sport,
He's a dad,
Who always spares a thought.

He's a baggie,
He's a die-hard fan.
He goes to every game,
If he can.

He looks after me,
And gives me treats,
He plays football with me,
In the streets.

He loves my mum,
With all his heart,
But he used to be a bit of a tart!

He's so friendly,
He's so kind,
His family are always,
In his mind.

Ben Payne (12)

MY Dad - HE'S Not That bad

My dad is the best,
Although he is a pest.
He's my number one dad,
And he's not that bad.
He's so cool,
And he's not a fool!

I love 'im, I love 'im, I love 'im
Down to the bottom of my heart
He is the best dad,
And as I said earlier,
He's not that bad!
Honest!

Matthew Miller (10)

untitled

I love my dad
He is the best,
He stands out from all the rest,
He takes us out,
We have a good time,
We go to Blackpool.
Some people say your dad's nice,
Your dad's cool
But most of all he's my dad
And he's the best.
Happy Father's Day.

Deborah Martin (13)

My Dad is ...

My dad is the best,
The best of all the rest,
He always has a smile to see
And he keeps one especially for me
If I didn't have my dad
I wouldn't even just be sad
'Cause my dad is the best
The best of all the rest
Yes my dad is the best!
Yes my dad is the best!

Rhiannon Heaven (9)

'RESPECT' TO Dad

You're a dad who sleeps and snores
You're a dad who loves his sport
You're a dad who loves to laugh and grin
You're a dad who's tall but very thin.
You're a fan of football
But you're a fan of Arsenal
And you're a dad who cooks and cleans
But most of all you're a dad
Who's good for help
Happy Father's Day!

Lolade Akande (12)

Dad

Father's Day is here again
Dad, he's smiling once again
Off to the pub he will roam
Don't smack his bum! Don't send him home,
It's Father's Day, he'll have his pint
He works so hard all the year through
Caring and sharing, hammering and sawing
That too,
But down your tools and wash your face
Nice to see that smile on your face
He's all dressed up, he sings his songs of Irish lullabies
Of days, of long
He's happy, he's smiling, no work today
Off to the pub he'll go - happy on his way
So if your dad should dare to roam
Don't smack his bum! Don't send him home
It's Father's Day for dads everywhere
They give us love and they do care.

Amanda Coughlan (11)

My Dad

My beloved daddy
You are always there for me
When I'm sad or happy
You share with me every moment I go through
Although I know that sometimes
I make you so angry
I also know that
With one little 'soppy' you'll forgive me
You care and love me
You don't care where or whom
You always show affection to me
You make known that I'm your
Only and beloved daughter
You call me all kinds of names
One finds rare to hear
My life, my aspirations, my vision
All of these, you shared and motivated
I love you my daddy
You are my strong pillar, which I lean on
My courage and my forever confidence
Forever I know that I can trust you
In all circumstances, bad or good
I love you my dad and you love me
Let's cherish our love and be happy always!
I love you my dad!
Many can be fathers but few can be like you!

Mercy Grace (14)

My Dad

My dad tickles me and makes me laugh he's also very funny.
I'll never forget my dad anytime at all.
Nearly all the time he gives me pocket money
And also he takes me to football lessons,
He buys me lots of presents.
My dad makes me feel happy inside and funny
And pleased that I've got such a special dad on the outside.

Gaby Taylor (8)

My Dad

My dad is one of a kind,
You can ask him anything,
And he can always make up his mind.

My dad likes his car,
He also likes rallying,
And he can drive his car near and far.

My dad likes to have fun,
And he likes to go on days out,
And he likes to go out in the sun.

That's what my dad is like,
And one last thing,
He has a motorbike.

Aimee Hadman (12)

Dad

My dad is my mate,
Especially when he lets me stay up late,
He lets me on his bus without any pay,
I can ride around on it all day.

We always play games together,
No matter what the weather,
I usually get beat, except when I cheat.

My dad is just great,
He'll be home soon and I can't wait,
So I'll be standing at the garden gate,
His bus is always on time and that's the end of my rhyme.

Callum Jones (9)

To My Dad From My Heart

When a child shouts *Dad*
In a public space
All the men with children
Think of their little younglings growing up.

Father's Day is a time to say thank you
For all those fathers out there
This poem is from a loved heart of a child.

In the world is only one
Sorting out antiques is what he's done
He started from zero and he's my hero
And this is the end of my rhyme.

To my dad from my heart (Nicholas)

Nicholas Nicolaou (13)

My Dad

My dad's brill, oh what a thrill
Home at last no shadows to cast.

We go to the park up with the lark
Football or slide, Dad's by my side.

We talk boys' talk, we walk boys' walk
Weekends are best the family's at rest.

'Have a good day,' he will always say
Sunday's no work, I'm never naughty, he'd go berserk.

Out on his motorbike or for a long hike
The time goes so fast when you're having a blast.

He never puts the hoover round but Mum never makes a sound
'Clean your room,' he will say; Dad I always will obey.

Sometimes we fall out and boy, can he shout!
But he kisses me goodnight, then there are no more fights.

My dad is the best dad ever
Our love no one can sever.

Adam Hughes (9)

Dad - Haiku

Dad, you are the best
So enjoy your special day
Like none of the rest.

Helen Schmidt (11)

Oh Dad

I love the way you talk to me when you're sat in your chair,
I love the way you laugh when we make jokes about your hair,
Oh Dad,
I love the way you drive your car and beep to all my mates,
I love the way you call some singers, eg Gareth Gates,
Oh Dad,
I love the way you kiss goodnight before I go to sleep,
I love the way you hold me close at bad times when I weep,
Oh Dad,
I love the way you don't get mad when I do something wrong,
I love the way you inspired me to write this rhyming song,

Most of all I love how you respect me, Dad,
You're the best I ever will have ...
And the best I've ever had.

Samantha Bannister (13)

untitled

Me and my dad are great as a two,
A trip to the park or a trip to the zoo.
He's always there to watch over me, if I get into trouble,
Or stuck up a tree.
I don't know why but he always seems to be right,
Except for that hairstyle (now that is a fright).
He knows everything my dad, maths, English and IT,
How does he know it all?
It's a mystery to me.
Then late at night when the sun has rest his head.
He'll say, 'Come on you, time for bed!'

Jamie-Leigh Hughes (14)

Darling Daddy

He is big and strong,
He loves me no matter what I do wrong,
Always caring and kind
He knows when I'm worried and says, 'Never mind.'

We go for long walks,
And he listens while I talk and talk,
Then he gives me a cuddle
Or tries to push me into a puddle!

We have so much fun,
And think about all the things we have done,
So on Father's Day, darling Daddy,
I would just like to say
I love you very, very much!

Rosie Ives (12)

My Dad

I love my dad, I really do,
If you knew him you would too,
He makes the world a better place,
And puts a smile upon my face,
When things go wrong,
And I feel so sad,
I know I can rely on my wonderful dad
So I'm writing this poem because I wanted to say,
There's no one like my dad,
He's the best in every way.

Sophie-Ellen Merrick (8)

Happy Father's Day

Father's Day comes only once,
Once in a year is a far too small time
For me to let you know
How much I really care for you.
It should come every day -
Just so I can hear you say
'Thanks for such a brilliant day!'

On this day made just for you,
I want to - in a special way -
Say to you 'Happy Father's Day'.

If only you'd not gone away
And still been here to hear me say
On your unique and wonderful day;
'I love you, happy Father's Day'.

Mallory Thorpe (15)

Dad's The bEst

Dad's the best, better than the rest,
Dad's so cuddly but very muddly,
Dad likes chocolate bars and also likes cars,
Dad's a loony and he likes a movie.
I love my dad and I'm glad he's mad.

Stephanie McGreevy (10)

NUMBEr onE Dad

Dad you're great and you're my best mate,
You're my number one dad
You're the great big lad,
You're the greatest even though you can be the latest
You're my number one dad
You're my number one dad
That no one could ever replace.

Sarah Tough (11)

My Dad

My dad is ace,
He is not good in a race,
My dad is great,
He lets me stay up late.

He drives a motorbike,
He is so funny,
He is like a fluffy bunny,
The best dad in the world.

Adam Jones (12)

untitled

My dad rides a motorbike
He rides super fast
It's a Honda Fazer
He thinks he's a born racer.

My dad is great
Lets me stay up late
He never shouts
Cos he loves me.

My dad is like a piggybank
He gives me money
He is very funny
Like Sonny out of 'Happy Gilmore'.

Jasmine Williams (12)

i Have A wonderful Dad

I love my dad,
And he loves me.
We have a good wrestle now and then
But most of all we have a good cuddle.
My dad gives me goodies,
But he hardly goes to the pub's
So out of all this my *Dad's No One.*

Georgina Holmes (10)

All His Life He Supports Man City

Caring person
Family lover
Football supporter
Loved by his daughters
Protective carer
Money sharer
Best man
Man City fan
A catalogue to make me the world's best dad!

Coralie Barnes (11)

i LOVE mY Dad

He's
Kind
Friendly
Cheerful
Funny at times
There when you're happy
There when you're sad
One in a million is my dad.

Stefania Cerritelli (11)

untitled

My dad is tall
My dad is big,
My dad is funny
My dad is the best
Dad in the world I think.
He never shouts
He always laughs
He is big and hairy
And like a gorilla.
Everybody loves him,
Even my mom
I think he must be Number One.

Kayleigh Brough (12)

untitled

My dad is the best
My dad is one in a million
He looks out for me and cares for me
He is the best; well after all he is my dad.

Ellie Burns (9)

i LOVE Dad

My dad is the best,
He's always on the move,
I'll never let him go,
'Cause I love him so,
Two families he has
Keeps him on his toes
There is four of us kids
With our wants and woes
And 150 black and white females to be cared for twice a day
There may be all the rest of the world's dads
But he is just the best.

Heather Broome (10)

A Dad is ...

A dad is a person who is helpful and strong
Sometimes old but sometimes young
My dad lets wind out loud
But he's only embarrassed if he's in a crowd
Each year that passes I'm more glad
That more and more you're my *dad!*

Nicole Tapper (11)

Dad

Dad you're the best out of the rest
Dad you're number one because I'm your son
Dad you make me happy because you change my nappy
Dad you make me laugh because you lead me to the right path
Dad you married my mum that makes me so calm
Dad you don't need to pay because it's *Father's Day!*

Sukhpreet Bangar (9)

Only Dad

Craig Knights!
He's only my dad,
But somehow he makes me glad,
I don't know why, I don't know how.
But that's just it. Wow!

Roxy Knights (11)

Fantastic Dad

Dads are very special
They buy you lots of presents
They're very helpful
With your homework
Except the division and fractions.
Some dads are wicked like mine
But I bet they don't drive a lorry.

Joe Brunt (9)

MY WONDERFUL DAD

The world would be terribly sad,
If I didn't have my wonderful dad,
He is unique in every way,
And laughs at everything I say.
He likes to play with my toys
Even though they are not really meant for boys.
But best of all and what makes him so fine
Are his hugs and kisses and the fact he is all mine.

Maddie Cooper (10)

My Dad

From my first words
That lit his face
To sports day
And the father's race
From the first tooth
That he pulled out
To maths tests
Passed without a doubt
From camping trips
And outward bound
To special treats
For doing sound
From helping me
Connect the dots
To watching Taz
I love him lots
From seaside trips
With sand turtles
To foil frisbees
And bollard hurdles
From a cheerful face
And a helping hand
To being there
Dad, you're grand
From my best friend
And great mentor
My dad will come tops
For evermore.

Gabriella Ireland (15)

My Dad

Dads can be thin.
Dads can be fat.
I don't care.
I love my dad
He may be disabled,
Unlike some
I don't care
I love my dad
He may not talk.
He may not walk.
I don't care
I love my dad.
He plays with me and laughs with me,
Unlike some
That's one thing I like about him!
Well I like *everything* about him.
He may not do things
Unlike some
I don't care
I love my dad.

Ewan Gault (8)

My Dad

My dad is impossible to compare
Someone similar is completely rare
He's resolute and pre-eminent,
The best father that God could have sent!

My dad is exceptionally unique
Someone as remarkable is too difficult to seek!
He's humorous and intelligent
A person I will never resent!

But, I can't describe him perfectly with just one single word
An exact example I can't say that I have heard!
There are some, however that will be good enough to say ...

Have a happy Father's Day!

Holly Bailey (13)

whY i LOVE you DaddY

When I despair and all seems lost I'll think of you,
And when I'm near you I feel precious and I am your princess,
And the world is my throne,
A pulchritudinous being is released when I see you
And I feel wanted and special,
A jewel that only you spy what great value it holds,
You see my glistening colours,
You visualise a spectrum of colours overhead this timid girl.

You'll play with me when I'm alone,
And when I arrive home,
You're there beaming at me with a smile only fit for royalty,
I am royalty in your eyes,
And Daddy that is all I need to be happy,
I do not fret over others' thoughts for me
And only your precious contemplations,
You can take something simple
And transform it into something so indescribably beautiful,
And your works of art spread a warm sense of pride,
That I have achieved the beyond best daddy in the world.

You have filled the puncture in my heart from the loss of Mummy
And my tears evaporate when I think of you,
You have replaced something inside me that is always joyful,
And when your presence is near all senses disappear
And I can only grin,
All pessimism and evil is extinguished when you are with me,
I am beautiful with you
And your scent of lavender always stays with me.
And at night, I am swept into a blissful dreamworld
Where I will only ever be yours,
And this can only be with the reassurance that you are there,
Sleeping,
You compel me,
You complete me,
And Daddy that is why I love you.

Nikhila Patel (12)

To Dad

To the man in my life,
You Dad,
You give me comfort,
You give me warmth,
You give me everything a child would want.

As I grow up,
I thank you for everything.

From the ups and downs,
And good and bad.

Dad, you have good trusting honesty,
And can keep a secret,

So Dad can you keep this one ...

Just remember,
I'm still your baby girl,
No matter how old I am!

Emily Tune (13)

untitled

My dad is kind
Funny and cool
He makes me laugh
When he plays the fool.
He makes me happy
When I feeling down
He's my very own clumsy clown.

Chelsea Aitken (11)

My Dad is cool

My dad is cool
He makes me laugh
He has black hair
And a brown moustache
His chin is rough where his beard used to be
He tells me stories that are really funny
But the best thing of all as you can see
Is that I love him and he loves me.

Amy McLauchlan (11)

Daddy

The soot-black beard enshrouds the mouth
That creases with laughter
When regarding his little girl,
Attempting to hang her dolls clothes on the washing line.

The twinkling eyes glitter with mischief,
When watching his son putting sand in the water barrel.

The furrowed brow is tensed with concentration
Whilst his muscular arms try to wield the minuscule cricket bat.

The overwhelming love surrounds me
When he holds my hand in his.

Elizabeth McLaren (15)

My Dad

My dad is the best dad in the world
He is full of fun, he laughs and jokes
And that's why I love him so much.
He likes his footie, he always has a beer
When something good has happened
He jumps up with a cheer
He helps me when I'm down
He always has a reason to make a joke
And to make me laugh.

Abbey Guy (12)

Father's Day

The love I have for you Dad
Is special and complete
Because to me you'll always be wonderful and sweet
And now that Father's Day is here,
I'd like to send my love and cheer
On Father's Day you are the best
You're not like the rest.

Jamie Coates (14)

MY Dad

My dad was always there for me,
When I was down he was always around,
Now it's Father's Day I would like to say
Thank you for being a great dad all the way.

He sits on the coach snoring away,
Lying asleep all day.
Waking up cutting the lawn,
Nobody can take my dad's place
Knowing he's mine I'll never forget his face.

Kiran Dhaliwal (12)

My Dad's A Kid

My dad's funny,
My dad makes me laugh!
My dad's silly,
He's sometimes really daft!
My dad's playful,
He spends time with me all day.
My dad's special,
He's kind in every way!
But most of all I'd like to say,
I'm proud that he's my dad,
For he's the biggest kid a son has ever had!

Michael Goodger (12)

That's My Dad

Dads are cool as a block of ice,
They cuddle you when you're sad.
They're really fun to hang around,
A dad is what you can't replace,
They're really special cool and sweet as they should be,
Loveable as well,
The dad that I have is the best,
He's cute, sweet and all of the above.
That's my dad.

Jaspal Kaur (12)

Dad

Dad ...

You are there for me
To lend me a helping hand
When I'm unhappy
You'll listen and understand.

Special days we've had
Will fill my heart forever
Memories of times
We've shared together.

I've known you all my life
Seeing a familiar face
The laughter in your eyes
When you taught me how to tie my lace.

So, thank you Dad
For all you've done
You really are the best!
All through this poem I've been checking
To see if you've passed the test.

Larischa de Wet (11)

NUMBEr onE Dad

N o one like my dad
U nique and special
M emories of us spending time together
B rilliant for the latest news on rugby and cricket
E agerly listening to things I have to say
R ealising that he is a very exceptional dad.

O ne in a million
N ever leaving me out
E verytime including me.

D ad is extremely helpful
A lways helping me with my homework
D eciding what is best for me.

Alrich de Wet (9)

Dad!

Take us all over the place,
Fairhaven lake,
Beaches and fresh air.
Aftershave when he goes out ...
By the bucket load.

Never embarrasses me
He can be cool
Lorry builder by trade,
Hard worker
Plays football with me
Gives me time with him.
Trendy music,
Drinking beer (dances when he's drunk)
Hates motorbikes,
Will never let me have one.
Presents and pocket money,
His time is the best,
It is priceless
I want to be like him when I am older,
Kind and great
Sometimes tells me off (when I deserve it!)
Thanks Dad.

Kyle Danson (13)

My Dad

My dad,
He is magic
He wears a magic hat,
Blue baseball cap.
Just like me ...
Makes me feel safe,
He cares for me
Spoils me a bit ...
We both love games
The best dad,
Jason!

Zak Winkley (11)

ABout mY Dad

My dad is like a bigger version of me,
A big broad grin but no freckles,
Scent of blue jeans when he goes out
Bike and black uniform at work
Most of the time he's great fun,
Only bad tempered when pushed!
Taking me to football, linesman for the team
High hopes for us all, a great dad
Looking after me, looking out for me
Wanting the best for me
Dad Michael Brogan!

Daryl Brogan (11)

MY Dad

My dad always takes me to Blackpool every Sunday,
Going on all the rides!
He plays football with me at the park every Tuesday.
He's busy but he makes time for me.
Working hard and going to colleges
A good example to us all,
Fairhaven Lake for fun at the weekend.
Fishing and ice creams for everyone.
Lynx when he goes out ...
By the bucket load
Visits Mum at work and does the shopping,
I can tell he likes to be with us,
Tickles me to death.
A great dad, Mark!

Jake Danson (11)

untitled

This is a poem about my dad and he isn't that bad
He takes me out and we have lots of fun under the sun
Here we go off to see the show
Out of the gate we'll be home late.
We went to the fair and met Claire
My dad's cool and no tool
So boys go away cos he's here to stay
We do everything together and we'll be friends forever
Me and my dad.

Rebecca Mossop (11)

untitled

My dad is the best,
So much better than the rest,
He gives me lots of money,
And he is rather funny,
He takes me on holiday
And I hope he's here to stay,
I really do love my dad.
Without him I'd be sad.

Megan Blackburn (12)

Dad

My dad is the greatest, the greatest one there is.
He comes out and plays rugby with me
And then goes to get some fizz!

My dad has only got one leg and one leg is not enough
So when it's cold, wet or rainy he always feels kind of rough.

But I love my dad I love him with all my heart,
So when he finds out what I've done he'll think it's really smart.

My dad's my hero and my superman.
And 'cause he's Scottish and I am half
The best clan is the Drummond Clan.

Happy Father's Day.

Harry Drummond (11)

Oh Dad

Oh Dad
You love me when I'm bad
Oh Dad
You comfort me when I'm sad
Oh Dad
When I do wrong you never go mad
Oh Dad
You gave me things I never had
Oh Dad
You are a good lad
That's why I'm proud for you to be my dad!

Tosin Taiwo

My Dad

My dad is called Neil
And I think he's great
He's got twinkly eyes
And he's my best mate.

He teases me sometimes
He can be a pest
But I really don't mind
Because he's the best.

If he wasn't my dad
I'd be very sad
My sister and I shout
We love you Dad.

Jade Hustler (8)

MY Daddy

My daddy is great
He loves me loads
He is my best mate
I love him loads.

He is helpful and kind
He is the best in the world
He works very hard for his two little girls.

Eleanor McCabe (6)

My Dad

My dad is tall, he is cool
He's got a six-pack and he rules
He loves boxing he hits the bag hard
I love him so much I will buy him a card.
My dad is like a hedgehog he's got spiky hair
He is special he is very rare
My dad supports Wolves, he loves football
If you want a game of footy give him a call
My dad is mid-thirties you know what they say
In a few years he'll be going grey
My dad is brilliant he is great
He loves his work and is never late
My dad is clever he is bright
Everything he does is also right
He likes Buttons, that's my cat
He likes animals but he doesn't like rats.

Daniel Clayes (12)

My Dad

In whose arms did I sit and curl?
My dad
Who cheers me up when I am sad?
My dad
Who picks me up when I fall down?
My dad
Who buys me sweets as end of week treats?
My dad
Who helps me with my homework when I am stuck?
My dad
Who sticks up for me when I need help?
My dad
Who loves me more than anyone?
My dad
Who is the best person in the world?
My dad
Who's the luckiest girl in the world?
Me!

Priya Mann (10)

My Dad!

My dad is the best,
He never needs to rest,
He's always on the go,
Even when I don't know.

From when I was a baby
And sitting on his knee
Up 'til now, when I'm 10,
He's not like any other men.

So that's the poem
That describes my dad,
He's always been like this even when he was a lad!

Faye Hodgson (10)

Dad

Our dad is great,
He works really hard,
Sometimes until late
There is my twin brother and I and four more sisters,
He loves us all the same,
He is not very tall but the best things are only small,
We all love our dad.

Alexandra Maguire (10)

Father's Day Poem

To some people Father's Day is just another day.
Some people are lonely and depressed,
Whereas other people are not,
Father's Day can mean a lot of things
For example, celebrating you have a dad,
But for some, that can only be imaginary,
Writing this poem has shown me to be thankful of my dad's interest,
To take note of what he asks me,
And to make him proud of me whatever I do
There are people out there, who don't have anyone,
Which makes me extremely thankful I have a dad.

Samantha Dolan (12)

Dad

(This poem is fictitious)

Dad! What a wonderful word,
To me it sounds so absurd.
I've never had a proper dad you see,
At the pub he'd always be.
Until one day my mum got sick,
And up the bum she did kick.
Out the door she sent him flying,
That was the beginning of all the crying.
Instead of sitting feeling blue,
In comes daddy number two.
Daddy two was rather weird,
With anorak and shaggy beard.
It didn't last it's fair to say,
His obsessive train spotting got in the way.
Mum promised there would be no more,
Then came the knock at the door.
How silly could she be?
In comes daddy number 3.
Times were good for a while,
But sure enough he went the mile.
No more dads it's fair to say
All these men have turned mum gay!

Lucy Hutchinson (14)

my Dad

My dad never lets me down
He has the sense of humour of a clown
He is always wearing his best smile
It reaches across the world for miles because ...
My dad is one of the best dads in the world!

Kacie-Kimie Shanks (11)

My Dad

My dad's name is Pete
He has very smelly feet
His favourite meal is mince and rice
I think my dad is very nice.

My dad likes to watch the telly
Laughing makes him wobble his belly
My dad is very kind
He's the greatest you can find.

Hannah Wilkinson (7)

MY Dad is mad

My dad is rather ugly
He really looks a fright,
But underneath his painful looks,
He's a big delight.

My dad is very funny,
He makes me laugh and laugh,
He always walks around the house,
Acting rather daft.

One day my brother came back home,
It was very late,
He'd just been babysitting,
For some food he couldn't wait.

Then Dad came naked down the stairs,
And wrestled him to the ground,
Dad sat on his head and said,
'I'll get off for a pound'.

So there you go, in 16 lines
I've summed up my dad
And the reason that I love him is,
I'm just like him, I'm mad!

Conrad Godfrey (12)

i LOVE mY Dad

I love my dad
He's gentle and kind,
Whatever he does,
Is rightly inclined.

I love my dad,
He's caring but fun,
He helps with my homework,
He is as bright as the sun.

When we won the cup,
My dad was here,
Whenever we scored,
Dad gave a cheer.

I love my dad,
It's clear to see,
The best thing though,
Is I know he loves me.

Sarah Loughran (11)

ThE OnE AnJ OnlY

You know my stepdad he's the best,
He is way better than all the rest,
He's soccer mad, how I'm so glad,
That he is my kind and wonderful dad.

We play football together
No matter what the weather,
On Father's Day he will see,
Just how much he means to me.

I'll remember all the time,
All the obstacles that he's climbed,
To make my life happy and fun,
You know my stepdad, he's number one!

Jordan Davids (10)

mY Dad

My dad is a very good dad; he's very loving, caring and kind,
And if we have a play fight he really squeezes me tight,
Sometimes at bedtime, when I'm not tired
And don't want to go to bed
We have a little wrestle then it's lights out, goodnight.

When we get up for school and it's breakfast time
Dad's not usually at home, he's long gone before 9
Then when I get home after my school day is over,
My dad's already home and he's waiting for me to play.

Time at home after school is not very long,
I've got other fun activities to do,
Football, swimming and kung-fu with Dad, then the day is done,
Bedtime is here again and its time to sleep,
When I wake in the morning Dad will be nowhere to be seen.

I'm never worried in the morning when I wake and my dad has gone
I know he's at work and later will come home to me,
Tonight when Dad came home from work,
He had great news for me,
He's got all next week off work so it's off to the beach for me.

Alex Chadwick (8)

My Dad

My dad's name is Jase,
He brought us up in a great place
Dad comes home with money,
Then he found his honey,
We began a new life,
And his honey is becoming his wife,
His favourite singer is Akon,
And he absolutely loves bacon,
His parents' names are Frank and Shelia
They taught him to become a second-hand dealer,
His daughter Aimee has a very big gob,
So he works long hours at his job
He's got two sons, me and Kyle,
Sometimes he says we can be vile
He can sometimes be a fool
But I think he's quite cool,
Dad also now has got three stepchildren,
Ash, Danielle and Charnee
With six children I think he's gone barmy
With his hair turning grey
But that's OK.
Finally at the end of the day I'm glad
Because he really is the best ever dad!

Jacob Mainwaring (12)

DadJEctiVES

(Words That DEScRiBE ThE TWO SidES of mY Dad)

Serious: Funny
Sad: Sunny

Generous: Mean
Reluctant: Keen

Patient: Rash
Sensitive: Brash

Great: Small
Modern: Neanderthal

Grumpy: Cheerful
Brave: Fearful

Strict: Easy-going
Boring: Mind-blowing.

Naomi McAdam (10)

ballad of The imperfect Dad

The imperfect dad is almost always late,
Making a million by his fortieth was simply not his fate.
He can't do maths or algebra, so homework help is out,
Patience is a virtue, but it's one he was born without.

The imperfect dad isn't funky, cool or hip,
(He thinks Bill Gates invented the oven microchip)
But he can repair any gadget underneath the sun,
And he dismantles oily engines just for fun.

The imperfect dad forgets to pay pocket money,
But his Mr Bean impersonation is rib-ticklingly funny
Supermarket shopping is one of his pet hates,
He'd rather potter in the bike shed, chattering to his mates.

The imperfect dad's a chronic hypochondriac,
With arthritis, tennis elbow and a dodgy back
But he's everybody's gofer, not to mention unpaid chauffeur -
No wonder sometimes he collapses comatose on the sofa.

The imperfect dad rejects all healthy food,
Gorges on doughnuts, drinks beer (is sometimes rather rude).
He's super glued to a TV remote (like all regular guys),
And he tapes Schwarzenegger movies over Mum's 'Desperate Housewives'.

The imperfect dad's himself - he's never fake or cheesy;
Doesn't pretend to be Superman, or make gestures just to please me.
My *perfect dad*'s ideal, he's really good at heart,
He may be just like Homer Simpson, but I'm a clone of Bart!

Shane McAdam (15)

Daddy's girl

I love my dad he is the best
He cheers me up when I'm depressed
He's always there to help me out
He's really nice even when he's cross
I love him lots
Thank you Dad for being there
For loving me, always.

Rebecca Hall (14)

untitled

Brave my dad is,
Interesting he may be,
Love he gives to us all,
He always plays with a ball,
He might be tall,
Round or bald,
But he will always be my pal.

I will never find a better dad than my own,
If I didn't have a dad like I do at home,
I would be with someone else,
Or on my own.

Aidan Romero-Muñoz (9)

Daddy

What a blessing!
What luck!
What fortune!
What an opportunity to have a father like my dad!
You that shows me the way to go.
You that tells me tirelessly the way to success is hard work
Dad you are the best dad.
In you Dad I see the man in me
You that is very quick to hear but slow in speech,
You that is full of wisdom
You that your fair sense of judgement save me and my younger ones a lot of
    disagreement
I love you
You are a gift of love to me
I love you Dad.

Okude Oluwatofunmi (9)
All Saints Church School, Nigeria

My Dad

My dad, my dad
Babajide is his name
And business is his game.
Boff and Co is his company,
Boff and Co is where he works.
With his developed brain,
He makes money.
With also four kids and a wife to care for
He still co-operates well.

Dependent on God and raised as a Christian
Four sisters and parents also in life.
At the age of forty-seven,
Still up and running.
Getting older each passing day.
Since eighth March 1958 still alive,
He owes it all to his Creator.

With his black eyes he sees everything,
And with his hands he works day and night 24/7.
With a kind and generous heart like his,
No one would want any other kind.
The life of Babajide Olatunde-Agbeja,
Has not ended,
Instead it has just begun.

It takes a lot of guts
To become a man like -
Babajide Olatunde-Agbeja.

Oluwaniyi Olatunde-Agbeja (10)
All Saints Church School, Nigeria

Dad

My dad is my male parent,
As gentle as a dove.
He is very kind and loving.

He asks for my problems.
And gives me encouraging words.
He pays my fees and cares how I feel.

He looks after his family.
He works for dawn to dusk.
Just to see that his family is comfortable.

Oh what a worthy person you are
I appreciate all your effort.
My precious dad.

Olanrewaju Omowonuola (9)
All Saints Church School, Nigeria

My Dad

My dad is like the sweet jewel of the Savannah
He does everything in the best manner
When over all I come out as the best,
He gives me a present
There is no one that has the best dad but me.

Tito Moyela (8)
All Saints Church School, Nigeria

MY DADDY

The caretaker God gives me to
To take good care of me
To teach me the way of my creator
My daddy

He imbibed into my behaviours
The doctrine of God
That I should rather please God, than man
My daddy

My mentor, role model
Who sat and watched my infant head
When I was growing from a baby
My daddy.

Suliat Oyinkansola Giwa (10)
All Saints Church School, Nigeria

MY Father

My father, my father,
What a loving and caring father,
Who can sell his last tie to meet the need of the family,
His counsel is full of wisdom that brings relief
And joy at the point of trouble,
His loving stories are educating, you'll laugh,
Laugh and laugh when he is more precious
Gold is precious, my father is more precious than gold
I love my father, oh my father, I love him.

Olabode Adebayo (10)
All Saints Church School, Nigeria

My Daddy

Daddy! One out of millions
Working all day without rest
Sleeps late in the night and
Still wakes up early in the morning

He does exercises and sweats all day.
He provides some money for Mummy
To take good care of the children

He is a hater of evil and
A lover of God
Despite his tight schedule,
He still finds time for his home and children.
What a kind and loving father I have
Oh! What a pity he is working again!

Babayode Oyinkansola (9)
All Saints Church School, Nigeria

My Father

Father oh father, a man filled with energy and tolerance
Hard-working and honest
A young bright man of 36 years old
By name Toluwalope Afonja, born in Akure, Ondo state
Resplendent rainbow in the sky,
How your magnificence makes me sigh
On you, all beautiful colours confer a well-deserved honour
A true puzzle of my life
Thanks father for the promising future you always make me long for.

Afonja Kanyin (10)
All Saints Church School, Nigeria

My Dad

There is always one man or the other;
To admire I confess.
There is always a pet of special interest;
To be glad to identify with.
The object of admiration to me,
Till tomorrow of course is the handsome man,
That hails from Ikire, Osun state, Nigeria.
The gentle man is about 5 feet tall,
Tender and loving to me and all in the home.
He took my mum honourably to the altar,
Ten years ago or thereabouts.
Then solemnisation of marriage blessings commenced.
To God be the glory we are five.
Too wonderful and amazing is God's hand on my dad.
Too many fathers out there are nuisances.
To care for and nurture their families is a taboo.
Too busy somewhere else to be responsible,
'Tangible' excuses, complaints and immaturities
Truncate them from the most noble assignments.
Tireless and never bored is mine
To mum's, my other sister and brother's problems
Those too great for him he took to God
Together with us and sometimes alone.
Throughout my lifetime, Dad, I own you thanks and gratefulness
Time and chance will always be favourable to you and yours.
Things will forever go on well with you and your reliable God.
Till at least we are also bigger,
Than you to offer more important legacy,
To generations yet unborn.

Kolawole Praise Mololuwa (8)
All Saints Church School, Nigeria

My Father

My father, my father
My father is my mirror
Whenever the mirror breaks
My father is gone

My father, my father
My father is my second God
Whenever he talks
I must surely obey

My father, my father
My father gives me one thing
Which is the king of all
My education.

Adesope Adejuwon (9)
All Saints Church School, Nigeria

My Daddy

When I am in need of my father
He is there for me
He teaches my homework
He corrects me when I am wrong somewhere
He cares for my needs
I love my daddy
Without my daddy I can't live
Because of my daddy and God
That is 'why I am alive'
I love my daddy.

Pelumi Abiona
All Saints Church School, Nigeria

My Father

Oh! A very dear father
My dear loving father
Very caring and compassionate
Warm and understanding
Correcting yet loving
A great man indeed
Always there to be leaned on
A man so much cherished by his children
My father
Oh! My father
A loving man, who can find?
I can
That's my father - my mirror.

Denloye Olaoluwa
All Saints Church School, Nigeria

mY FathEr

I love my daddy
I love my daddy
He is tall and very slim
He takes me to school every morning
Buys me snacks and picks me up in the afternoon from school
Buys me ice cream on sunny days
Makes sure my homework is correctly done
Instils discipline in me
Encourages me to read newspapers and listen to news.
Shows me the way of righteousness
Teaches God's word that I may not perish
Gives me presents to encourage me in my academics
Teaches me how to love God every day.

Collins Akinade (10)
All Saints Church School, Nigeria

My Father

Dad, you are the most handsome man
I have ever seen on this Earth.
Dad you are so kind to me, loveable dad, you're loving to me.
You are the dad that shows love, kindness and gentleness to me.
Dad I know you really like me, you provide for my needs and my school needs
Dad I love you so much, because you care for me always.
You care for our demands, Dad I love you so much, and I wish you to live long
You are so much, I pray you can see your great-grandchildren
I know if you see them you will be very kind to them
Oh, Dad I really like the way you look after us.
Dad I have never seen a man like you.

Titilope Adeoti (10)
All Saints Church School, Nigeria

MY Daddy

My father is a priceless gift.
A rare gem among men,
Men do not translate to it automatically.
Fatherhood and responsibility are inseparable.
I cherish the qualities and characteristics found in mine.
I have had the privilege to be in contact with people,
But the greatest influence has come from my dad.
My father, a structure an architectural pattern I follow in building my greater tomorrow.
My father's strong character base for commitment and dedication
Has been an emulation and driver to live an honest and delightful life.
My father means more than I can write,
His name is Modesty and his is the model on my life.

Diala Blessing (9)
All Saints Church School, Nigeria

my Dad

My dad, my dad
I love my dad
So loving and caring
So intelligent and faithful
Everyday you shine to me like a bright morning star
A day without you is like a day with nobody
Your love for me cannot be hidden
How I love you dad
How I love him.

Gbadero Pelumi (10)
All Saints Church School, Nigeria

my Father

I love him so dearly.
Daddy cares for me.
My daddy provides our needs.
I love my daddy so dearly.

My dad.
My loving dad who cares for me
Pays my school fees
Provides good shelter because he is the head of the family
And he is so loving and kind that he is my sweet daddy.

Feyisayo Hamilton (10)
All Saints Church School, Nigeria

My Father

My father, my father
A very nice and kind father
The best of all
What will I do without you?

My father, my father
You help me to study well
And help me to treat my wounds
A very great dad indeed!

My father, my father
When you are not around I feel very sad
You are the book in my education
The person I even resemble

My father, my father
You care for, not only me but the whole family
How I wish you could stay with me forever
A very great dad indeed!

Oluwaseun Fayiga (10)
All Saints Church School, Nigeria

my fatHEr

My father, my father
So caring so kind
My father, my father
So handsome, so precious
When I see you, you are like a star
When I see you, you are like the moon
When I see you, you are like the sun
My father, my father
So caring
So kind.

Oyinloye Ibukun (9)
All Saints Church School, Nigeria

mY fathEr

My father,
My father,
The best father the world has ever seen,
Loving and caring,
Mild and gentle,
Cool and caring,
He can do all things to meet the need of his family,
What a loving father.

Ojekunle Damilola (13)
All Saints Church School, Nigeria

My Father

Dear Father, I love you so much
You're so good to me
Dear Father, you paid my school fees
You brought me to life
You correct me when I am wrong
You provide for my brothers and me
You gave me education so that I can shine above my mates
Oh Father, Father how loving you are
Oh Father, Father how caring you are
God bless you Father.

Ayomikun Taiwo
All Saints Church School, Nigeria

MY Daddy

My daddy is a tall man.
He is fair in complexion with a lot of grey hair
My daddy loves and cares for me.
He shows me love both when I am good and naughty.
He wakes me up at 6.30am so that I won't be late for school.
He drops and picks me at school everyday so I don't walk home.
When I get good grades he congratulates me.
He tells me to work harder when I get bad grades.
He advises me on what to do and not to do.
My daddy is my hero.

Agboola Demilade (9)
All Saints Church School, Nigeria

my Father

Dear Father, dear Father
My father the precious father
The father who cares for his family,
The hard-working and understanding father
The loving and caring father the devoted father.
The father who helps his fellow human beings
Whether bad or good.
My father is very generous and he is the best
Father a family can get.

Oladipo Bateye (11)
All Saints Church School, Nigeria

my Father

My daddy what can I do without you?
When I am down and lonely you are always there for me.
You are the mirror, which I see my future in.
My daddy without you I can't be where I am today
Is it my school fees that you pay every term?
Or the food that I eat every day or the shelter I live in,
So Daddy what can I do without you?

Pelumi Oni (9)
All Saints Church School, Nigeria

My Daddy

My daddy
O loving Daddy
Early morning star
Glamour light
The beginning of life
The breadth and length of the family
The Alfa of me
Kind and care for me
O Daddy you are great
Dark and tall, young Daddy
Ebony and smiling face
Action Daddy
I will never forget a great achiever
Like my daddy, Stephen Ewubajo.

Dolapo Ewubajo
All Saints Church School, Nigeria

My Father

Oh my dear father
How wonderful you are
He loves me always
What a loving father
I love you

Oh my dear father
So compassionate and loving
So kind and generous
You are caring like a mother

Oh my dear father
I know you are a Christian
You help me out of trouble
What a caring father.

Olamide Opatunde (11)
All Saints Church School, Nigeria

my Daddy

My daddy is my male parent
Through you I was brought to life
You are as quiet as a dove
You take good care of me
You are nice and loving
You take good care of your family
You are as nice as dove
You help me when I need help
When I ask you to help me in solving problems
You are there to help me
You provide all my needs
Just to make me happy
When I am sick you are there to take good care of me
You are the best daddy in the world
I love you Daddy
God bless you
Amen.

Adenike Rachael Ajuwon (9)
All Saints Church School, Nigeria

mY FathEr

My father, my father
You brought me up so well
That I cannot imagine
You taught me many things
How I wonder
How is your thought?
How is your mind?
You are so brilliant
That I cannot imagine
Oh! My sweet father
You are so wonderful
My father, my father.

Chukky Eribo (9)
All Saints Church School, Nigeria

MY DADDY

My daddy is a pastor
I love my daddy
Because he is a hard-working man.

He loves children
He likes to sing
He likes to pray.

He is a caring daddy
He is an honest man
And kind to me.

Joy Akinbiyi (9)
All Saints Church School, Nigeria

A POEM For My Dad

I taste your taste,
When I bite into a piece of toast.

When I hear Mozart or classical music in the shops,
I think of all your CDs and you asleep in the chair listening to them.

When I see packs of lagers piled up in Asda
I think of you opening a can.

When I see the keys hanging up,
It reminds me of you losing your keys.

When I watch GMTV
When I am flicking through the channels
I think of you watching it at 6.00am,

I can see you running downstairs
In the prison to an emergency,

You make me laugh,
When you wear two jumpers and jeans, over and over again.

You make me happy,
When you take me to lots of dog shows.

When I smell your Lynx deodorant,
I always know you have been in the bathroom because of the smell.

I love you because you are my dad.

Hollie Graham (10)
Eagle Community Primary School, Lincoln

My Dad

I can picture you playing the guitar and
Shouting at Bri when I look at you,
I can see you when you are marking papers for work
I can see you at work when I go in your room and see your lecture notes
I can hear you when I listen to U2 or Downhere
I watch you all day making a guitar out of an old one,
Or tapping your hands against the steering wheel.

Crisiant Williams (9)
Eagle Community Primary School, Lincoln

My Dad

I taste your taste when I eat an Indian takeaway,
It reminds me of us two watching a good movie on Friday evenings.
I listen to you when the alarm goes off for work,
Or when you're singing one of your George Michael favourites.
I see you in your polo shirts and this reminds me of you in your blue shirts for
   work.

I feel the tennis ball beating at my racket every 2 seconds
I love you like you love our new house,
This reminds me of you teaching me football, which you love most,
I sense you when you're happy winning an over 35s trophy!

I taste your taste when you're drinking your wine,
This reminds me of us two eating at a beautiful restaurant,
I see my mum's phone waiting and hoping for a text from you.
The touch of a soft sweater reminds me of you.
I feel your hands on my back hugging me,
I feel like I never want to let go.
I love you Dad and I would never want to lose you!

Ivenna Durmush (10)
Eagle Community Primary School, Lincoln

My Dad

Every morning I taste your great boiled eggs
I hear you turning up the volume full blast, when Oasis comes on.
I hear you crunching on your cornflakes early in the morning
Before you rush off to work.
    I love you because you're my dad!

I hear you dropping your keys as you jump out of the car
Shouting at my brother when he does something wrong
Your loud chuckle when you see something funny.
    I love you because you're my dad!

I taste you when I smell burnt toast that you are making for breakfast
I sense the speed of your motorbike
With its revving engine taking you to work
I see the pots sparkling after you have washed them.
    I love you because you're my dad!

I taste you when I'm eating beans on toast - your favourite meal!
I hear you on the buzzing computer keeping me up all night
I jump up and hit the roof when you come home
    You are my dad and I never want to lose you.

Jack Turner (9)
Eagle Community Primary School, Lincoln

mY FarMing Dad

I hear you moaning when the sheep gets away and laughing when I am daft.
I smell you when we have been shearing and all the grease is on our trousers
I see you smile when you have bought more sheep from market.
I love it when you make up funny rhymes,
I hear you saying that border hog, she's covered in wool
And just back it up a bit when we are working with the tractor.
I think of you when I see a livestock lorry
When I see a buff Orpington chicken,
I think how much you love the breed
I taste your taste when I taste a good joint of beef.
I see you when you have come in from lambing.

I love my farming dad.

Jack Battersby (10)
Eagle Community Primary School, Lincoln

My Dad

I hear you revving your motorbike to warm up the engine.
I smell your deodorant in the morning drifting through the house.
You are the best dad in the world.

I hear your car starting up when you are going to work.
I see you in your jeans and T-shirt
You are the best dad in the world.

I can hear you on the phone telling my mum you are getting better
I see you getting out of the ambulance to come home.

I hear you singing to Nickleback, which comes on the radio
I smell Bolognese when it wafts that you have cooked.

I see you crying when Aunty Margaret died
I love you and I don't want to lose you.

Adam Gidley (10)
Eagle Community Primary School, Lincoln

My Wonderful Dad

I know when you're here because I smell the strong aftershave
I get mad when you switch on the radio
And listen to talk sport because it's so boring!
I know when you're around in the mornings
Because I hear you chewing and crunching cornflakes.
When I touch a hockey stick I always think of you
I taste your taste when I eat Mum's shepherd's pie
I listen to you when you explain something to me so I can learn.
I see you in a photograph as an amazing hockey player.
I know when you're back from work
Because I hear your car engine coming noisily down the drive.

Sam Perrin (11)
Eagle Community Primary School, Lincoln

My Wonderful Dad

I see you,
Covered in grass after cutting the lawn
It reminds me
Of you and I at an agricultural show or market
I listen to you when I hear the doorbell ring and I know it's you
I see you in a photograph taken when you were younger
I know you can be disappointed and furious like a four-stroke motorbike
I taste your taste when I collect a free-range egg from my chicken.

Ryan Sturges (11)
Eagle Community Primary School, Lincoln

ThE bESt DaD in ThE wOrld

I taste your taste when I eat roast beef and Yorkshire puddings.
I hear you come back on your scooter from PJs,
Working on the production line
When we go to aeroplane shows,
I can see you flying so high wishing we could buy an aeroplane strip
When we go to the Toothill farm
I can feel you inside milking the cows
When I hear you playing the guitar
I wish I could play it like you and with you!

Jane Elliott (10)
Eagle Community Primary School, Lincoln

my Dad

I see you when I listen to the Scissor Sisters on the radio or on a CD
I cry for you when I see a photo of you holding me as a baby
I hear you when the phone rings,
Rebecca answers and her voice turns high and happy.
I smell you when I smell the strong scent of coffee
When I get a text from you,
I clench my phone tighter wishing you were here
The one day a month when I see you,
I'm in heaven just seeing your face
When you're embarrassing
And run through town or dance in shops to music you like
Dad, the one-day a month is just not enough
I wish you were here everyday.

Charlotte Clarke (10)
Eagle Community Primary School, Lincoln

ᴍY Daᴅ

I hear you when I hear somebody doing the gardening
I can smell you when I smell Lynx the deodorant
I feel for us both as we share the same interests
I laugh with you when you tell funny jokes
I know you as being a hard-working welder
I listen to you when I hear your car pulling up
I feel proud of you when I hear about your achievements.
I am happy when you congratulate me on my trampoline skills
I am safe when your arm is around me.

Shelby Ward (10)
Eagle Community Primary School, Lincoln

My Dad

I see your pride in the Aston Martin you drive on special occasions
I hear you dad making funny noises and being stupid on the phone
I smell the scent of your Gucci aftershave drifting through the house
I hear you coming in late from the pub.
I see the look on your face when you see what Mum
Has put on your plate and you had wishing you had eaten out.
I thank you Dad for getting me involved in so much sport.
I see the victory of your racing in your eyes.

Thank you Dad your number one.

Jack Thompson (11)
Eagle Community Primary School, Lincoln

My Dad

I have a dad, who is like no other,
He chases me around,
Until I run for cover,
He tickles and teases
And pinches my sweets,
And so I call him 'cheesy feet!'

He takes me on bike rides,
And tells me they're fun.
But when I come back, I have a sore bum!
He tries to do the housework,
In the absence of Mum
But dusts around the ornaments,
And tells me to keep stum!

He's quite bad,
And a bit mad,
But no one could ever replace my dad!

Gemma Fisk (11)
Gawthorpe High School, Burnley

My Dad

I love my dad with all my heart
He lives in Whittick with Diane where I go to visit,
But tears roll down my cheek when we are apart
My dad is funny and full of energy
And that's what makes him my number one dad
But I don't need to worry
Because I know he is in safe hands
With the best stepmum ever
My dad is tall with brown hair and brown eyes
Just like me
That's what makes us a perfect match as dad and daughter
And that's why he means everything to me!

Kirsty Keegan (12)
Gawthorpe High School, Burnley

My Dad

My dad is so cool
My dad is the best
My dad can play football
I think he's the best.
He's better than my brother
He's better than my mum at football
But most of all,
He's the best dad in the world.

Gemma McIntosh (12)
Gawthorpe High School, Burnley

my Dad

I don't have a dad
And I am very glad
But when my friends visit their fathers,
I feel all alone and sad,
When I have to stay at home
I dream about him often
And wonder what he's up to
In my head I have my perfect dad
And that's the way I like it.

Rebecca Bond
Gawthorpe High School, Burnley

My Dad

My dad is happy and never sad
He takes me to places I like to go,
I'll ask for things he'll never say no.
Because my dad is the greatest ever,
And he will be here forever and ever.
When we go out I'll get what I want,
If he can't afford it he will just say I can't,
But that doesn't really matter.
Because my world won't shatter.
My dad is the best, make no mistake about that
Even though he can act like a 'prat.'
But that's my dad and he will always be,
My dad, my sister, my brother and me!

Melissa McVay (12)
Gawthorpe High School, Burnley

i LOVE mY Dad

I love my dad,
He loves me,
We play together
In all weather
Wind, rain,
Sun, snow.
Whatever the world
Will throw at us two
We will both get through.

Beth Ashton (12)
Gawthorpe High School, Burnley

untitled

My dad is so special,
He could soar among the birds
My dad is so special
I can't describe him in words
My dad is so special
And he has so many friends,
My unconditional love for him,
Will never ever end.
My dad has not much hair,
It's not long, wavy and curled,
But it doesn't really matter,
Because he's the best in the world.

Sarah Longworth (12)
Gawthorpe High School, Burnley

My Dad

You can be a bit irritating
But that makes you seem more elevating
You are bright, intelligent and sensitive
You're never too tired for teasing me.
I find your funniness mad.
But you're still my dad
My sisters and me love you the way you are.

Imogen Siddall (12)
Gawthorpe High School, Burnley

My Dad, my Dad

My dad, my dad, he is so cool,
He is handy all around the house.
He's always found with his tools,
But can be as quiet as a pygmy mouse!

My dad, my dad, just like Del Boy
Not only just in name.
He does not sell dodgy stuff,
But he can certainly call your bluff!

My dad, my dad, a lover of music,
Queen, Elton and The Stones too.
But one thing is very basic,
He absolutely hates the modern era ... poo!

My dad, my dad, his sense of humour,
'Monty Python' and 'Little Britain',
'Spitting Image' and maybe 'The Simpsons'
All of these he'd wish he'd written!

So ...
My dad, my dad he is so cool,
My dad, my dad: He rules!

Andrew Bragg (13)
Glenthorne High School, Sutton

Dad

My dad makes me laugh because he's funny,
Rain, hail or snow, especially when it's sunny.
He is always there for me when I'm down,
He cheers me up by acting like a clown!
We like to watch films on Saturday night,
Especially the ones that give you a fright.
A person who is there for me
And jokes that aren't too bad,
I'm glad to have, such a great dad!

Sara Druce (13)
Glenthorne High School, Sutton

POEM ABOUT MY Dad!

This is a poem written in May
For my dad called Ray
The one true friend, I ever had
This is for you my special dad.

In the past through thick and thin
I forgive you for your sin
You have been my hero since Year 1
One more verse and then we're done

You're the one we love with our heart
With every single body part
The one true friend I ever had
This is for you my special dad.

Matthew Ashby (13)
Glenthorne High School, Sutton

MY Dad

My dad is really funny
My dad is really cool
When I'm feeling lazy
He drops me off at school

My dad is really crazy
My dad is really mad
My dad will give me cuddles
When I am feeling sad

My dad is really special
In every single way
He will always be the best dad
Every single day.

So now it's nearly Father's Day
I'd really like you to hear
I love you Dad you're the best
Every day of the year!

Hayley Cahill (12)
Glenthorne High School, Sutton

My Dad

My dad Paul,
He drives me up the wall,
He is big and strong,
He is tall and long,
And loves his football.

He makes me laugh,
And calls me a giraffe,
He is silly and loud,
He is great and fab,
And he makes me very proud.

At times he makes me mad,
At times he makes me sad,
He is great and fun,
Like an ice cream bun,
Proud to have him as my *dad!*

Louise Scott (11)
Glenthorne High School, Sutton

my Dad

My dad, his name is John,
He likes having fun,
Out with his mates,
Down the pub,
Never in a nightclub,
He goes skiing,
His mates always give him a ring,
He drives a train,
This keeps him out of the rain,
He is getting old,
And he loves the cold,
He likes to cook food,
And he is very good,
I love him like mad,
Because he is my dad!

Sam Webb (12)
Glenthorne High School, Sutton

FathEr's DaY

My dad has got a bald patch on his head
And when the sun comes out it goes very red
He works and slaves on cars all day
But the fat on his tummy does not wear away.

He takes me for my swim
And won't let me give in
He likes updating my computer
And fixing my electric scooter.

He can give us all a good laugh
But sometimes he can be quite daft
The reason why we have Father's Day
Is to thank our father for his way.

Clarissa Baker (12)
Glenthorne High School, Sutton

FathEr's DaY: mY Dad

My dad works hard
Six days a week
And needs to take a break
On Sunday he spends time with us
From the time that we're awake.

Dad is the best in the world
And loves me and my brother
He is kind and loving to both of us
Even when we are in bother.

I love my dad, he is the best
Even when we fight,
He takes me out, buys me stuff
He's fair; he's more than alright
He's my dad.

My dad works so hard
That he comes home and sleeps
He will never take a break
We do not see him until 9 o'clock
And this is a poem for you
I love my dad!

Sean Doncaster (12)
Glenthorne High School, Sutton

untitled

When I am in need
My dad to me is a friend indeed
A friend to talk to
A friend to talk with
A friend
A father
That's what my dad is to me
My dad isn't like other dads
Who don't really care
My dad isn't like other dads
Who sits in a chair
When I am in need
My dad to me is a friend indeed
A friend to talk to
A friend to talk with
A friend
A father
That's what my dad is to me
My dad isn't like other dads
He didn't abandon me
My dad isn't like other dads
He is always there for me
When I am in need
My dad to me is a friend indeed
My dad isn't like other dads
Because he belongs to me.
Happy Father's Day.

Chelaynie Barnes (12)
Glenthorne High School, Sutton

Father's Day!

My dad is not just any normal dad
My dad is the best of all
My dad goes out sometimes and has a couple of beers
My dad has not got big ears
My dad does all the DIY
My dad is quite shy
My dad is fun and he loves my mum
My dad is the best!
So as you can see my dad is not just any ordinary dad
He is the best of all!

Happy Father's Day!

Kirsty Ashby (12)
Glenthorne High School, Sutton

Father's Day

My dad is the best
I love him so much
He is so groovy
I think you are the best.
Don't you worry you'll be fine
You're always there
That's why I'm saying
Happy Father's Day.

Lotty Creates (11)
Glenthorne High School, Sutton

A POEM FoR Dad

A poem for he is as busy as a bee
Can you guess who he is?
He's not a Mrs or a Miss
He's a Mr, my father
Full of laughter
My father has care
Like a big cosy, warm bear
My father has love,
One hundred times more than a dove
My father is a real man
He likes to be shown on his webcam
My father is a number one dad
He's never ever bad,
My father is a number one dad
He's never ever mad.

Akeem Howell-McKinley (12)
Glenthorne High School, Sutton

mY Dad

My dad is fun he really is great
He is not good with time so he is often late
We like to play and skip and run like.
Like I say my dad is so much fun.

I worry sometimes and hide my toys
He thinks he's still one of the boys
He is not good in the morning
So on his door there should be a warning

My dad thinks he's hard because he's a joker,
But there's one thing about the rude boys
They're all smokers.

What I like about my dad is that he makes things fair
Even though he can't store anything in his hair
Because nothing is there.

In this poem my dad may be stupid and funny
But I love him, I love him because he has lots of money.
I'm joking, I'm joking I love my dad through the world and back.
That is no lie but I will always love my dad
Till the end of the day and long after I die
And that is a fact forever and ever and ever.

Charlotte Puddy (12)
Glenthorne High School, Sutton

POEM For Dad

My dad gets up early in the morning,
Has a shower and still is yawning.
My dad is a builder he works with bricks and cement,
When he takes his break he is always sent,
To get the lunch for everyone else,
But never has time to eat food himself.
He comes home always tired but still watches TV,
My dad's a drummer in a band called 'Junk Time Party'.
My dad watches 'American Chopper',
He has a big fat belly like a space hopper.
When he says he's going to bed we say OK,
He wakes up in the morning and starts a brand new day.

Riccardo Dipalma (12)
Glenthorne High School, Sutton

My Dad

My dad is the greatest
He's the best in the world,
He could beat all the other dads with one eye open,
My dad is the greatest.

My dad is the greatest,
He's brilliant at golf,
Just one swing and it's in the hole,
My dad is the greatest.

My dad is the greatest,
He's brilliant at singing,
When he's singing as Neil Diamond,
He sounds like the real Diamond,
My dad is the greatest.

My dad is the greatest,
Even in years to come,
When he's old and grey,
My dad will still be the greatest.

Sam Liddle (12)
Glenthorne High School, Sutton

MY POEM ABOUT Dad

My dad has blue eyes that shine in the night,
Although he's wrong, he thinks he's always right,
He thinks Chelsea are simply the best,
And says they're better than the rest.
My brother disagrees, he thinks not,
He likes Arsenal a lot.
The computer is something he hogs,
And he's a very big fan of dogs.
He loves to watch his team play,
Who thrash Arsenal every day.
He plays football every Thursday,
And his rest day is every Sunday.
He fights with me all the time,
But wouldn't dare to commit a crime.
But you're my dad,
And I like you the way you are
Thanks for being
My dad
I love you and no one can take your place!

Siobhan Drewett (13)
Glenthorne High School, Sutton

Dad!

When you used to go away,
I used to say, I wish he would come home today,
Sometimes you can be a grump,
Sometimes you can be sad,
But you are always glad,
When I come home and tell you what I've done,
When we go fishing together,
I just wish that day would last forever,
When you work in the garage,
You make me work hard,
You may be short,
But you were good at sport,
When everyone used to shout,
You always went to sort it out,
All I'm trying to say is,
Thank you for being,
My dad!

Garreth French (13)
Glenthorne High School, Sutton

My Dad

Ever since I was little you have been there for me
When I was sick or I fell over
You would give me a hug and make me feel better
I would wake up in the middle of the night and shout for you
You would give me a hug and make me feel safe
You would sit there and tell me the stories you wrote about me
Until I drifted away into my dreams.
Although I am older I still love to spend quality time with you
It is never hard to find something to talk about
As we share the same interests.
You are handy to have around the house
And you can do nearly any job.
You're a whiz at helping me with my homework
And you're the best cook in the house
You're exciting and fun to have around
And you come to my rescue when there is a spider around
Although we have our arguments I can't not talk to you
As you always seem to get me to talk.
We always seem to think the same things
You're always there to listen
Dad all I am trying to say is that you are
The best dad in the world
And I wouldn't change you for anything.

Kate Rose (13)
Glenthorne High School, Sutton

ᵐY Daᵈ!

I love my dad
He is a great lad
He is a funny
As a bouncing bunny
He is very cuddly
And he is lovely jubbly

My dad is exciting
But can be very frightening
Sometimes he shouts
When I am out and about
He makes me sad
And I start getting mad

My dad likes going to watch Chelsea
And going down Selsea
He is very caring
And he likes sharing
My dad can be very crazy
But most of the time lazy

My dad has dark brown eyes
Which remind me of pork pies
He has dark brown hair
Not like mine 'cause mine is fair
He is quite tall
Unlike me I am short
It doesn't sound like he should be my dad at all

I love my dad
He is a great lad
He is a funny
As a bouncing bunny
My dad is very cuddly
And he is lovely jubbly.

Paige Arnold (13)
Glenthorne High School, Sutton

My Dad

My dad is a footie fan,
He watches it whenever he can,

He's a proper armchair supporter,
When it's on I hate being his daughter,

At the end of the season he seems a bit down,
Until I persuade him to treat me in town,

To make him feel a bit more low,
I go shopping and spend loads of his dough,

You might think this is mean and hard,
At least he has forgotten about yellow and red cards,

This might not last long but I do what I can,
At the end of the day, my dad is a footie fan!

Becky Greenham (11)
Glenthorne High School, Sutton

Daddy i LOVE you

Father, Father I love you, I've loved you as I came through,
I picked you; you're the perfect one,
All of us daughters see it from the sun.

I love you and you love me,
We're a happy family with a great big hug and a kiss
From me to you, won't you say you love me to.

I see you in the morning,
I see you in the night
I see you in my dreams, kissing me goodnight.

Lauren Gripper (12)
Glenthorne High School, Sutton

Sorry Daddy

Sorry Daddy that I shout
Sorry Daddy that I let my anger out
Sorry Daddy I can't control myself
But I do wish you were here when I'm all by myself.

Sorry Daddy that I'm not always kind
Sorry Daddy that I sometimes lose my mind
Sorry Daddy that sometimes I'm annoying
But I know you're glad and happy when I give you a ring

If I could change one thing about me it would be that I was caring
If I could change one thing about me it would be that I was loving
If I could change one thing about me it would be that I didn't have a temper
If I could change one thing about me it would be that I was a normal family
    member

If I could change one thing about you it would be that you didn't shout at me
If I could change one thing about you there would be no I but we
If I could change one thing about you it would be that you were twenty-eight
If I could change one thing about you I'd change nothing because you're great.

Lucia Fagan (11)
Glenthorne High School, Sutton

My Dad

My dad is wonderful
In millions of different ways,
Helping when I need him
He listens when I talk
He picks me up and holds me tight
And says 'Everything will be alright.'

He's always there to guide me through whichever path I take,
And I want to thank him for being there each and every day.

I love you Dad!

Alice Bennett (11)
Glenthorne High School, Sutton

My Dad

Even though my dad thinks he is the best at football,
I personally prefer Frank Lampard!
Nevertheless, I still love my dad
And nothing will change that!

Even when I'm naughty,
He will still give me money!
Only 'cause I'll bug him
Every minute of the day!

He's really quite a joker
And makes all my friends laugh!
He cheers me up when I'm feeling sad,
Then embarrasses me to make me look bad!

His favourite team is Chelsea,
He's supported them all the way!
All I want to give him,
Is a perfect Father's Day!

Kelly Angell (12)
Glenthorne High School, Sutton

FathEr's DaY

My dad is the best in the world,
My dad is the best, better than the rest
He makes me laugh, we are a team.
My dad supports the blues, Chelsea they are the best
You are the greatest dad
You play with me and do things for me
You are the best
When I'm upset you comfort me
My dad is reliable as he is never late for work.
He is mature too, well most of the time anyway,
My dad is a person, a friend and a father to me.
He is funny, playful and fun to be around.
My dad is the best in the world.

Megan Nichols (12)
Glenthorne High School, Sutton

Dad

F or every loving hug when I was feeling down
A nd every caring world to make a smile of a frown
T ears and laughter in the rain and the sun
H oping, with each other, we could overcome
E very problem that may come our way, I
R eally don't know what I'd do if you ever went away
S o I pray, with me you'll always stay.

D ays like this
A re created to say
Y ou are the greatest dad ever, in every single way.

Lauren Goldsack (12)
Glenthorne High School, Sutton

MY Dad

My dad is the greatest dad to me
And I'm sure your dad is greatest to you,
But there's something special about each of our dads
Mine is that he'll always be there for me.

All the time people say my dad is
Better than yours,
But that's your opinion,
No one else cares,
Except for your brothers or sisters.

If you've been bad or naughty you
Might feel to scared to own up,
But don't keep it inside just tell your dad,
He won't get mad,
But that's my opinion not yours.

I love my dad, he is one of the most important things to me,
He comforts me when I'm sad or blue
He always makes me feel better,
I hope your dad does the same to you.

My dad is great even when we argue,
I love him the same
Although I may not feel it the love still runs through my veins.
That's why I love him so much.

My dad is the greatest but that's my opinion not yours.

Catarina Brodziak (11)
Glenthorne High School, Sutton

POEM For Dad!

Dad you are funky,
Dad you are cool,
I like it when,
You act a fool.

You always buy me presents,
You always buy me treats,
You always buy me chocolate,
And instead it's sometimes sweets.

Sometimes you get stressed,
Sometimes you get mad,
But you never really tell me off,
When I do something bad.

Dad I think you're wicked,
Dad I think you're great,
You're the best at being a dad,
And the best at being a mate.

Kyra Sutherland (11)
Glenthorne High School, Sutton

My Daddy

My daddy takes me everywhere
To Chelsea, Park and Golf everything
We do together we always have a laugh,
He works very hard to give me what I would like,
He says I'm too expensive and I should take a hike,
We sit and talk and have a bond, which will be there for life,
Until I'm older and then I'll take a wife,
My daddy is the best,
Better than all the rest.

Sam Burroughs (12)
Glenthorne High School, Sutton

My Dad

My dad is so cool,
He is the best dad that rules,
We have good cuddles,
Even if our days are in a muddle.

My dad is a plumber,
He likes the sunny summer,
He likes to do funny things,
Like having fancy telephone rings,
I can tell he loves me,
Because he has a face of glee.

Emma Clayton (11)
Glenthorne High School, Sutton

My Dad

My dad doesn't play premier league football,
He can't play tennis at all.
He might sit at home, and watch rugby
With a mate and a beer, on the TV

He'll listen to cricket scores on the radio
However, to ice hockey games – he won't go.
But get him in the garden with
My brother and me
And suddenly ...

... He's
Wilkinson
Henman
Or even
'Young' Rooney!

Lewis Metz (11)
Glenthorne High School, Sutton

My Dad

I am glad to have a dad because my dad is the greatest.
He buys me lots of things like expensive clothes and diamond rings.
My dad is very cool and his favourite sport is football.
The good thing about my dad is that he is expensive but fab.
My dad likes to eat pies and I like to buy him brand new ties.
My dad works very hard and he acts as my bodyguard.
I love him lots and that's no lie, when I am around him he makes me fly.
He takes me out to expensive places and buys me lots of trainers with laces
I love him lots and that's a fact, even though he cannot sing or act
He supports Spurs, and they are the one that he prefers.
I love him lots and he loves me, except for the fact
that I am a *shopaholic!*

Charley Larkin (11)
Glenthorne High School, Sutton

Dad POEM

Dad, you're always there for me when I'm down,
You're so special you deserve more than a crown,
I just want to say how much I adore you,
But many words cannot assure you.

You'll stay with me forever in my heart,
And I hope we will never drift apart,
You can always guess when I'm sad
Because you are the world's greatest dad!

Dad, your smile is great,
It is something you just create
I love you dearly Dad you're more than my mate,
You're my lovely father that no one could hate!

The touch of your hand makes my world expand,
The step of your foot makes everyone look,
The sound of your voice makes me know I have a choice,
The sight of your eyes makes me know that you're wise,
And you Dad, you're the best!

Roxane Moylan (12)
Glenthorne High School, Sutton

MY DADDY

My daddy is the nicest dad,
The nicest a little girl could have.
He's loving, kind and definitely caring,
He thinks of me a lot and is always sharing.
He is quite tall and is lots of fun,
We like playing games, especially in the sun!
He has thick, black, curly hair,
And to me he is my giant teddy bear!
He has a good job and gets paid lots of money,
And to me, well, he is quite funny.
No matter what, he is always happy,
He's my daddy and he always will be.

Jennifer Smith (12)
Glenthorne High School, Sutton

Father's Day Poem

We laugh together when we're happy,
You're there when I am sad,
So I just want to say you're the world's best ever dad.

I love you lots, with all my heart,
You and me will never part,
You're always there for me when I need you,
I'm always there for you when you need me,
You kiss me goodnight when it's time for bed,
I lie down silently and rest my head,

You're funny and smart,
You'll never let me down,
When I'm sad and look at you with a frown,
You comfort me and I comfort you,
I know you love me and I love you too,

So now all I want to say is *I love you!*

Jenny Hill (11)
Glenthorne High School, Sutton

Dad

My dad is the best
He helps me not like all the rest
My dad is really real
He taught me all my football skills

Everyday I learn from him
He always makes me laugh
Everytime we go to watch Chelsea
He makes me wear my scarf

My dad is the best in the world
He's worth more than gold
Even if it was for platinum
He wouldn't be sold!

Luke Foulsham (12)
Glenthorne High School, Sutton

FathEr's DaY pOEM

My dad's really special
I'm sure that you would agree
I wouldn't say that he's perfect
But he's the best one for me.

Ohhh this is a Father's Day song for you
Dad you're so special and
I wanna find ways to say I love you.

Sometimes he gets grumpy
And sometimes he gets angry
But I still know that he loves me
And that I'll never forget.

My dad's really special
I'm sure that you would agree
I wouldn't say that he's perfect
But he's the best one for me.

Joshua Ogenyi (12)
Glenthorne High School, Sutton

POEM ABOut mY Dad

My dad is the best
He's very cuddly
He loves to play
But gets annoying

He is very caring
But hates animals
He helps with homework
And is very technical

He likes the TV
He likes to watch the Grand Prix and 'Star Trek'
As well as supportive and very playful
But likes to relax

He would love to win the lottery
So he didn't have to work
He's not that lazy
But likes a lie-in

He likes to play badminton
He likes it even more when he wins
He gets stressed easily
When my sister and I argue

He is lovely and caring
And has a heart and that is my dad.

Megan Akers (12)
Glenthorne High School, Sutton

i LOVE my Dad

I love my dad and that's no lie,
I buy him presents like a brand new tie!
I love him so and that's a fact,
Even though he cannot act!
He buys me lots of things,
Like shoes and diamond rings!
He is very hard-working,
But he doesn't like gherkins!
He gets lots of money,
And he is very funny!
My dad is one in a million,
Trillion, trillion, billion!
He is my dad,
If he wasn't I'd be sad!
He is the best,
Better than the rest!
He's never grumpy,
Only when his custard's lumpy!
He supports Liverpool,
'Cause he thinks they are cool!
He likes his books,
But doesn't concentrate on his looks!
When I'm with my dad I feel like I can fly,
That's why I love my dad and that is no lie!

Jenna Poulson (11)
Glenthorne High School, Sutton

POEMS For Dad

A dad who's the king of the family,
As marvellous as Christmas Eve,
As quick as a Concorde,
As strong as a wrestler,
A dad who's braver than the police,
As funny as a clown,
As quiet as a ghost,
A dad who's as busy as a bee,
As bold as a fried egg,
As clever as a clog,
As sporty as a sportsman,
A dad who's cheerful as a cherry,
As caring as a nurse,
And that's my splendid *dad!*

Jay Patel (12)
Glenthorne High School, Sutton

MY Dad!

He was the first to hold me
when I was a baby.
Whenever I want something,
he always says maybe.

He taught me to swim
when I was six,
and how to amaze everyone
with magic tricks.

He's taken me on holidays
from Cuba to Greece.
Whenever I'm cold
he lets me wear his fleece.

It's always an adventure
wherever we go.
To fun on the beach,
from playing in the snow.

Whatever I do I always
make him smile.
It's got me thinking
for a while.

Forget Paul, Steve,
Dave or Trevor,
I know that my dad
is the best dad ever!

Abbie Studholme (13)
Glenthorne High School, Sutton

My Father

My father is a merchant,
He gives me words of gold,
Feeds me juice with wisdom,
Gives me air with hope.
His hands have a touch of love,
He gives me mouth fulls of laughter,
And grins and smiles and frowns.
He rights me when he knows I'm wrong,
And though I feel he's not correct,
In the end it works.
My dad loves and cares,
I always frown at what he does,
Though he does it all for me.
I know my dad will find it hard,
He'll have to set me free,
But I know I'll make it through,
'Cause of what he's taught to me.
I'm grateful that my father's here,
To guide me through each and every year,
To make sure that I'm alright.
Our dads are why life is life.

Loise Madete (12)
Greensteds School, Kenya

Dad!

Dad
I think
You to me
Are the best dad
That there has ever been.

Dad
I want
To tell you
How brill you are
And you are never mean.

Dad
I need
To let you
Know that you are
Like a great big star.

Liam Connor (10)
Leys Farm Junior School, Scunthorpe

My Dad

My dad is the best dad in the entire world,
He always helps a lot when I'm in trouble and getting beaten up,
He is a really wonderful dad,
He's got a really big sense of humour at work,
He plays with me and always helps me,
He's fabulous and looks famous and he is a good dad and the best dad.

Stephen Hutchinson (9)
Leys Farm Junior School, Scunthorpe

My Dad is irish

My dad is Irish he:
  Sleeps, sleeps, sleeps on a day off work
  He drives his car like a rally car;
  He wears long trousers and a button-up top;
  I think he is brill at hockey,
  He cannot swim, as he did not learn;
  I think my dad is quite mad when it comes to drinking and dancing;
  My dad goes to the beach with me and my bro and comes back as the sun's
  Hot, hot, hot;
  My dad is a nice man but not when he tells me off;
  But I still love my dad and no one can change that.

Liam Egan (11)
Leys Farm Junior School, Scunthorpe

Daddy

I am your number one fan;
Even though you do not have a tan.

No matter how much you cannot cook;
I'll still love you though your food is yuck!

You used to put me in my cot,
When you shout you lose the plot.

I still love you every day;
You're my father and you're here to stay.

Aisha Cooper (10)
Leys Farm Junior School, Scunthorpe

Dad

Dad always tells me off 'cos I always give him cheek,
He's always out to work trying to buy a Merc.
He's getting a motorbike so he doesn't have to hike
He likes building decking and if he does it wrong, he smashes it up!
He drives 130 mph - he's a nutter
I drive him crazy by:
- by being cheeky
- turning over the TV
- doing everything wrong
- not listening to him when he shouts me

But never mind, he's my dad and he's *great*.

Harry Wheaton (11)
Leys Farm Junior School, Scunthorpe

MY Dad

I love my dad lots and lots
He's always annoying me!

He has got a favourite jumper
Knitted by my nan!
He wears odd socks
And he smokes a pipe.

He thinks he's cool
When he is *not!*

He says he can drive
Mum says he can only drive
Her up the wall!

Even though he does all that
I love him lots because
He's my dad!

Emma Bradley (10)
Leys Farm Junior School, Scunthorpe

My Dad

If you meet my dad, you will surely see
He's the best a dad can be.

He's good at football; he's good at swimming
I think he's getting used to winning.

He's the best ever, and I will keep him forever.

James High (11)
Leys Farm Junior School, Scunthorpe

MY Dad

My dad loves for me and cares
So I want to win for him this bear.
Even when he is really busy
He makes time for me, even if he is dizzy.

He protects me from others,
Especially from my evil brothers.
They shout at me,
For standing in front of the TV.

I couldn't wish for a better dad,
In my eyes he is never bad.
Even though he's not the world's best cook,
I love him even though his cooking is yuck!

On Saturday he takes me to work,
Where there's just him and I stand talking while he works.
He means everything to me,
I wouldn't sell him for 50p.

He helps me with my homework
But he doesn't mind because it gets him out of housework.
My dad and me have many happy days together,
So I guess you know my dad means the world to me.
And is simply the best.

Ben Fletcher (11)
Leys Farm Junior School, Scunthorpe

COOKING mad Dad

My dad, he's obsessed with cooking,
He never leaves the kitchen,
Not even to place a bet.
He cooks cakes, steaks and maybe snakes,
He only leaves to watch the snooker and have a pint of John Smith's Lager.

I hope he doesn't stop cooking.
My dad he's just the best, the best I've ever met.

My dad he loves to drive.
At 100 miles an hour,
We have to hang on for our lives.

He wears his favourite shorts,
For 3 weeks at a time.
He's not as bad with his shirts,
He only wears them once.

Daniel Gorbutt (11)
Leys Farm Junior School, Scunthorpe

MY DAd LOVES ME

My dad loves me
And that I can see;
He gives me what I need,
When I was a baby, giving me a feed,
Up to today; where he cooks my tea,
For not even the smallest fee.

Joe Smith (11)
Leys Farm Junior School, Scunthorpe

My Dad

My dad is the best,
He looks after me,
Without any fuss,
He does things in a jiffy.

My dad is the best,
He helps me with stuff,
Without him around,
I wouldn't be able to do much.

My dad is the best,
Working at things,
He's the only one,
He's the best dad you've seen.

Catherine Larder (10)
Leys Farm Junior School, Scunthorpe

My Dad

My dad is cool, my dad is fun,
My dad makes me smile all day long.
I only see him once a week, but I miss him loads,
Then I'm happy when I sleep.

My dad is the best; he does anything for me,
Too bad he cannot cook tea,
I love my dad he's the best,
My best dad in the world.
I love you.

Georgia Blackley (11)
Leys Farm Junior School, Scunthorpe

My Dad!

My dad is the best in the world,
He can do everything cool,
He is not a poor mule,
He is really, really cool.

The sports he does are the best,
Such as rugby and cycling,
He is never up for a rest,
That is why he is the best.

When it's my birthday,
He buys me cool presents,
Chocolates on the menu,
Sweets and all.

When we are on the PC,
He challenges,
To a game of 'Call of Duty',
That is why he is the best.

No dad can beat my dad,
Because he is the best.

Daniel Bournes (10)
Leys Farm Junior School, Scunthorpe

My Dad

My dad is the best in the world,
He is funny and makes me laugh,
He does all of the DIY,
He always comforts me when I cry.

He takes me places to do fun stuff,
He never ever goes off in a huff,
He is terrific at trying tongue twisters
He gives me a plaster when I get blisters.

He buys me all the things I want,
Even when it's make-up!
He works in a metal workshop,
He only has one decent top!

I don't know what I'd do without him,
He has short black hair and a reasonable trim,
He is the best in the world,
And best of all he's my dad.

Hannah Smith
Leys Farm Junior School, Scunthorpe

My Dad

My dad is funny,
He's always there,
He's a very happy bunny,
My dad to me is a huggable bear,
My dad is the world's greatest dad,
My dad is cool,
But sometimes he gets a bit sad,
But my dad sometimes can be a fool,
My dad deserves this card because I need to say that I need you,
I love you and thank you for being my dad.
So happy Father's Day Dad.
The most important thing is that I love you and you love me.

Hannah Whitham (10)
Leys Farm Junior School, Scunthorpe

My Dad

My dad is the best,
He's sometimes a pest,
He goes to the pub,
To him, I'm his cub.

I love him so much,
I nickname him 'butch,'
He cooks like a pro,
He even kneads dough.

My dad is so cool,
He'd love a pool,
Me and my dad,
Want a big party pad.

Andrew Cromack (10)
Leys Farm Junior School, Scunthorpe

My Dad

My dad's the best in the world,
He buys me things,
He earns lots of money for us,
So now it's time to repay him.

He's cuddly and warm,
And he lets me play games on the computer,
He cooks my tea,
As he watches TV.

My dad's a supersonic man
He drives everywhere in his supersonic car,
But most of all he loves me and I love him.

Happy Father's Day Dad.

Abbey Kitson (10)
Leys Farm Junior School, Scunthorpe

Classical Dad

My dad is the coolest,
He plays with me every day,
He's tall, slim and muscular,
His hairstyle's quite OK.

It's a tremendously, large flat-top,
His occupation's good,
He goes and kills the gigantic fire,
Which I really think I could.

He's into 70's music
I don't like slow songs,
But there are always some good rockers,
The slow ones are always long.

The things he likes the best,
Are definitely classic cars,
At least over 40 years old
I like Jaguars.

Matthew Burridge (10)
Leys Farm Junior School, Scunthorpe

Untitled

F athers are so kind
A nd are always a step behind
T hey think of every little thing
H ow I wish that mine could sing
E very minute that we're apart
R eminds me that you're in my heart.

Lynn Smith (9)
Meadowburn Primary School, Bishopbriggs

Daddy

D ad's always making jokes
A lways having fun,
D escribing maths so clearly,
D ancing madly to U2
Y ou never know when he'll stop (having so much fun).

Ishbal Machennan (10)
Meadowburn Primary School, Bishopbriggs

Dad, Daddy ...

D ad, Daddy, Father, Papa you can call him any
A ctive is his game, Steve is his name,
D ecisions, decisions he makes the best
D octors who needs them, with Dad's magic powers,
Y ou need him, I need him, well I'm not sharing!

Heather Kindness (11)
Meadowburn Primary School, Bishopbriggs

FathEr

F aster than me,
A lways playing games,
T rying to help,
H elps me with my homework
E nergised and enthusiastic,
R esting, never.

Jamie Murray (11)
Meadowburn Primary School, Bishopbriggs

MY WONDERFUL DADDY

My dad is so very kind,
He always thinks of me in his mind.
He tucks me up in bed at night,
And lets me leave on my bedside light.
He helps me with my summer revision,
And then lets me watch television,
If I get a very good mark,
He'll take me to a water park,
I'm going to France with school this year,
And Daddy is paying, what a dear!
He said I can go skiing too
I think he's thoughtful, do you?

Sophie Holdich (12)
Oriel Bank School, Stockport

A POEM ABOUT MY Dad

My dad is the best dad ever, who lives in Southampton
Where it is very bad weather, he loves me very much.
I love him very much too, I want him to know.
He is the best teacher I know.
I hope he has the best Father's Day ever, I love him lots.
He's kind and loving, he loves and misses me,
He makes me smile.

Molly Taylor (12)
Oriel Bank School, Stockport

untitled

My dad is number one
Even though he can be dumb,
Sometimes he's sad,
And sometimes glad,
But the best thing is he's my dad.

He cheers me up throughout the day
Even when he's eating away.

Now it's night-time
We all go to bed,
But not my dad
He's still awake.
Doing what?
Watching football!

Sophie Cooper (12)
Ridgewood High School, Stourbridge

Action Man

My dad is a mega daredevil,
He jumps and he climbs and he falls.
But the *best* thing about him is ...
He's my dad!

He takes me climbing and abseiling too.
Jumping off cliffs,
Caving and camping on the beach.

He likes cycling, on his Santa Cruz
His football team is Leeds
Blue, yellow, white.

When I'm sad
He's a cuddly bear.
When I'm glad,
He's as mad as a hare.

But the *best* thing is ...
He loves me,
My family
And even ...
My sister.

Hayley Crump (12)
Ridgewood High School, Stourbridge

MY NUMBER ONE Dad

My dad, I can't explain
He's hopeless, but not a pain,
He's so hopeless it makes you smirk
As usual Dad shirks things like housework.

Without my dad I'd feel lost and alone
Like a dog without its bone
Or my mum without the phone
Or my sister without her moan.

My dad's addicted to football
Won't take his eyes off the screen at all
Villa are his favourite team
When they win it makes him beam.

Golf also goes down well
Last player usually rings a bell,
He's not really that bad
But when he wins he's really glad.

Cars though are his number one
He couldn't survive if there were none
He uses so much polish it makes me cough
Then drives around streets showing it off.

But at the end of the day
What more could we need?
I've got Dad
And he's got me!

Lauren Tibbetts (12)
Ridgewood High School, Stourbridge

MY Dad!

My dad's a Mr fix it
His name is such a hit
He's a 1 million pound film star
And owns a Citroen car
He love for me is great
He thinks of me as a best mate,
He chokes me with his hugs,
And buys me minging mugs
But overall he loves me
Now I can see
He's the best dad in the *world!*

Amy Law (12)
Ridgewood High School, Stourbridge

Dad's Poem

My dad is weird
My dad has a messy beard,
My dad's quite old at forty-eight
My dad he's like a best mate
My dad he likes rugby and seventies music
If I had the choice
I'd know whom I'd pick
I couldn't ask for more,
My dad is never ever a bore.

Elliot Partridge (12)
Ridgewood High School, Stourbridge

Dad

This poem is for you Dad;
You aren't that bad Dad,
You have a good sense of humour,
You like deadpan comedians,
Ronny Barker and co,
You enjoy watching Bond films, cooker and Grand Prix,
You train hard in karate and enjoy playing on lgl
You love going on holiday,
And surprising me,
And love spending time on the family,
You aren't bad
You're cool Dad.

Thomas Greensill (11)
Ridgewood High School, Stourbridge

This is My Dad

My dad is medium size with short black hair,
He always shows me lots of care.
He likes to fix things around the house.
He likes watching his favourite team,
To see England play in his dream.
He likes to sit down and have a rest,
He thinks his cheese sandwich is the best.
He looks after our local school,
To me my dad is really cool.

Nathan Potts (11)
Ridgewood High School, Stourbridge

untitled

I love my dad
But he drives me mad.
He's the best dad in the world
And he's always thrilled
He does support Wolves
Just like his son.
Without his kids
His life would be dull
He's not old
That's what I've been told
But he's my dad
Even though he drives me mad.

Carl Whitfield (12)
Ridgewood High School, Stourbridge

Untitled

My mum and dad,
Are the best thing I have.

Sorry Mum but this day is for my dad.
He takes me to the Albion
And on the PS2.

I always have the same dream
Me and Dad in the stream.

I love him dearly,
I love him lots.

Without a doubt
He's the best thing I have.

Jake Hill (12)
Ridgewood High School, Stourbridge

Thanks Dad

I love my dad
He's one of the best things I have
He is lovely and cuddly
He makes me feel all snugly.

He buys me the best clothes he can
But sometimes he tells me off, I get mad
He's so cool
I can't believe I'm saying it
But he's the best dad I could ask for.

But in the end he's my dad
And I love him as much as I can.

He is so so special
He's wacky, wonderful and wicked
He's definitely the number one dad!

Laura Vale (12)
Ridgewood High School, Stourbridge

FIVE SIDES OF DAD

Side one is cuddly
Number two is rather muddly,
Three is very lazy
Four is the one whose jokes drive us crazy
Finally is number five (This is my favourite)
It has all the love and pride,
Which he has inside.

Fran Wright (12)
Ridgewood High School, Stourbridge

Mad Dad

My dad is a load of fun
He enjoys relaxing in the sun
He loves to have a laugh
Even whilst sitting in a café
Birmingham City is his team
Whilst they're playing his eyes are glued to the TV screen
He has jet-black hair, bit of white here and there
He has blue eyes and never lies
Dad enjoys a doze
Put him to bed and into his own world he goes
My dad is so kind
My dad's always in mind
My dad is rather lazy
And now I think about it, also crazy
But I love my dad
Even though he's a bit mad!

Kelcey Lissemore-Secker (11)
Ridgewood High School, Stourbridge

ᴍY Daᴅ'ꜱ bEttEr Ɪhan ...

Sweets and chocolates lovely surprise
Watching favourite films on the TV
Things that make a loud noise
People buying things all for me
Things that smell very nice
Having the very best friends
Things that taste nice like rice
Hoping fun will never end
Making sure dreams come true
People who are happy and smiling
Everyone to live happily as they should do.
Been in front of everyone by a mile,
Having lots of friends who care,
Have nice clothes to wear
All these things are lovely but nothing
Is as good as my dad.

Bethany Ore (11)
Ridgewood High School, Stourbridge

My Multitasking Dad

Dad you are the best you can't deny
Even though you're a little shy
He gets home late from work tired
But all his work is desired
He cleans, he cooks, and he makes it clean
And loads the washing machine
That is my dad no one is better
And that dad will stay forever.

Beth Hart (11)
Ridgewood High School, Stourbridge

untitlE⅃

My lovely dad, he's kind and helpful ...
When he wants to be!
My dad tries to help but it just doesn't work, he makes a mess
I think, *what will he do next?*
The next thing I know he opens a beer,
Then gives a cheer, Leeds have scored but are 3-1 down
My dad can be confusing
Especially when Leeds are losing
He sometimes cares and then he ignores it like nothing's there
He makes me laugh when he's asleep and snores his head off,
It's really funny when he falls out of bed
I love my dad I truly do
But that doesn't mean I understand him anymore than I used to!

Laura Green (11)
Ridgewood High School, Stourbridge

untitled

You do care
All my secrets I can share
You're a big strong man
You're a football fan
You make us cry with laughter
No wonder we can't sleep after.

Daniel Jhalli (12)
Ridgewood High School, Stourbridge

A Fairy Tale

A poem about my dad,
Well what can I say?
He is perfect to me in every way.
There is not a moment throughout the day,
When he does not think of me,
When he wakes up in the morning,
And every day after tea,
When he is gone,
It's like there is something missing,
Like the circle is incomplete,
No bells are ringing,
Brown is his hair
However not so much anymore,
He's loving and giving,
Until his favourite team score,
My best friend he is
When we fight we will go on pretending,
The best dad in the world
My fairy-tale ending.

Emily Langridge (12)
Ridgewood High School, Stourbridge

My Dad!

My dad is the best
He loves fishing
He works as a builder
He puts himself to the test
That's why I reckon he's the best.

My dad, is adventurous
Right through to the bone,
I bet he would of built the Millennium Dome
He is six foot three tall is he
That's why I reckon he was in the navy
So that's my poem about the number one dad,
I hope you enjoy and it was not *bad!*

James Pardoe (12)
Ridgewood High School, Stourbridge

Daddy 'o' Daddy

You make me laugh
You make me smile,
I love you Dad
For more than a while,
I think you're nice,
I think you're sweet,
I love you Dad,
Don't make me weep,
I like your hair
I like your eyes,
I love you Dad,
Do you like mine?
You're so cool
You're so fine
I love you Dad
And do you like wine?
You're so happy
You're so kind
I love you Dad
If you don't mind
I always will
I love you Dad.

Hannah Price (11)
Ridgewood High School, Stourbridge

LOViNG Dads

Dads are sunny
Dads are cool
When you need loving
Just give them a call
He will come to you
And love you up
You just wait and I bet he will say
I love you so much.

Samantha Stock (12)
Ridgewood High School, Stourbridge

Dad

You make me laugh,
But never cry,
You make me happy,
But never sad,
When I'm in a mood,
You cheer me up.
You heal my wounds.
And bandage them up
You reward me with sweets if I'm good
Like liquorice, sherbet and candy bugs,
Time with you is precious like silver,
Spreading out wide like an open river.
Blond hair you have,
Blue eyes to see.
To get to you I'd cross the seven seas
So when you receive this poem of love,
I'll still remember you're big, strong and tough.

Alexander Brady (12)
Ridgewood High School, Stourbridge

A POEM For Dad

F un-loving and free
A dventurous is he
T ogether we make a great team
H appy for hours we sit and dream
E xciting and reliable he can be. The most
R emarkable man you'll ever see.

Douglas Partridge (12)
Ridgewood High School, Stourbridge

untitled

Dad loves cars just like me
Even if I leave home, my father he will always be,
Always there when I needed a cry,
Even if he couldn't help me he would always try,
He is like one big pillow,
Shelters me like a large willow,
Even though he's disabled he's the best,
He is better than all the rest
He loves Formula 1 and Moto GP,
Always there for me, he will always be.

Mark Clement (11)
Ridgewood High School, Stourbridge

grand prix Dad

Dad you're the best
Better than all the rest
You're always there for me
When everyone else is not,
I hope you stay with me.
Because you're the only one I've got
If I am lonely I know where to come.
You help me out when I act dumb.
You are very dear
'Cause you don't drink much beer
You watch the Moto GP
You watch it with me.

Alexander Johnson (12)
Ridgewood High School, Stourbridge

untitled

His job isn't the greatest
But I don't really care
All that matters is his character
He's kind and just and fair.

His mom is neck-down paralysed
And his dad is dead
But he takes life with a smile
And it all rolls off his head.

My father is a footy fan
But he hates the ref
He's the greatest dad in the world
And I'll love him through life and death.

Robert Malin (11)
Ridgewood High School, Stourbridge

HE'S FAB

He's fab
Because he's my dad
He's there all the time
He doesn't drink brandy & lime
But saying that, he loves his beer
But for him it is too dear
He reminds me of Homer
But he is not a loner
He's the top man in my chart
And he's very good at art.

Bethanie Lambert (11)
Ridgewood High School, Stourbridge

My Dad

He is the coolest, he is my dad
He is always acting mad
Fishing is his sport,
My dad proposed to my mum on Holyhead Port,
He is the best,
And thinks I'm always a pest,
He taught me how to ride a bike,
Then took me fishing and caught a pike.
He will always be the best to me
And you will always notice and see.

Josie Humphries (12)
Ridgewood High School, Stourbridge

untitled

This is to you, the one and only Dad
You got me through all the trouble I had.

I know you're mine; you're there all the time,
Waiting for me till you are 83.
So catch up with me then I'll be 33.

You gave me my presents,
You gave me all of those things
You buy me all them diamond rings.

Thank you for being there
When I am sick and sad.

You are the best dad I ever could have.
Love you!

Bethany Shields (12)
Ridgewood High School, Stourbridge

untitlEd

Thank you for being there when I am sick and sad.
For always caring and for always sharing.
For being there when I need you and for loving me dearly.
With a heart of gold you are the nicest thing this world could hold!

Happy Father's Day Dad!

Victoria Bennington (12)
Ridgewood High School, Stourbridge

untitled

Dad you may be a grumpy git,
Your belly has a six-pack (in your dreams)
You play games with me,
You think you're the best,
Apart from when you fall over your own feet!
Nevertheless that's what makes you my dad,
For your birthday you got a box at the races,
And a brand new set of golf clubs complete with bag,
Go to work every day at 8 and don't return till night.

Kloe Smith (12)
Ridgewood High School, Stourbridge

untitled

Dad, this is for you,
And everything you do.

You take me to all the football matches,
You stopped smoking for me with nicotine patches.

Your shoulder is always there for me to cry on,
You're like a star that's always shone.

You're the best dad by far,
And you have a nice car.

Charlotte Hudson (12)
Ridgewood High School, Stourbridge

ThE bESt DaD eVEr

My dad is cool, the coolest dad in the world
He is the best dad in the universe
He helps me when I am stuck
He cheers me up when I am sad
He always has time for fun!
My dad is the kindest man ever
He cooks, he cleans, and he is always fun
He does everything for us and not for himself
My dad is the best, better than all the rest
He takes us to wonderful places
He shows us new faces.
My dad always tries new things
He has a heart of gold
He will never lose it,
Even when he is old
My dad is the best dad *ever!*

Jake Cartwright (11)
Ridgewood High School, Stourbridge

MY Dad

You try to help me when I'm down,
Thanks for everything
You taught me how to ride my bike
And it was something that I really did like.
You really are a great builder
You could construct anything
You love your bacon sandwiches
And you try to bring me happiness when it's possible
You really are the number one dad and you make me glad.

Joshua Homer (11)
Ridgewood High School, Stourbridge

untitled

How did I ever learn to ride a bike?
How did I ever learn to kick a ball?
How did I ever learn to play tennis?
How did I ever learn to play racketball?
How did I ever learn to walk?
How did I ever learn to say, 'daddy'
I know by him himself!

My dad's emotions come right from the heart,
He's always there to have a laugh,
He's the greatest dad to ever have!
He'll always be my dad!

Olivia Emerson (12)
Ridgewood High School, Stourbridge

MY Daddy

All the time we spent together,
All the things we did together,
Was like the joy of a baby being born.
We are one great team, like an army of ants.
That's my daddy.
That's my daddy.

You were like a crutch when I fell,
And a shield when I was attacked.
When I learned to ride my bike,
And when we went for a hike.
That's my daddy.
That's my daddy.

Samson Reuben (13)
St Constantine's International School, Tanzania

A wonderful Dad ...

Oh Dad,
You mean a lot to me,
You are the one who loves me so much,
Sometimes I can't even understand your love,
You are the one who always gives me the right advice,
You made me what I am today,
You are the one who risks your life for me,
You are the one who I can't live without,
You are everything good for me in life,
God bless you, Dad,
Live forever,
Never leave my side,
As I won't leave yours,
You will always remain in my heart,
As a wonderful dad,
I love you so much, Dad,
I will never let you down,
Let us never quarrel in life,
Let us remain together in all our lives,
My dear, wonderful dad.

Hiten Dave (11)
St Constantine's International School, Tanzania

Dad ... My Friend

I sit by the greenery and think ...
I think of a friend, a friend who would listen,
Share my sorrow and grief as I cry,
A friend who would change the day with a smile.
And so ... I think of dad ... my friend.
Life is a roller coaster with high ups and low downs ...
Dad makes the high ups higher and the low downs search the ups.
An important friend is Dad,
Whom I carry in heart for all times,
Alas my thoughts have deepened into wishes and I forgot ...
That time is not available, not for me, not for my friend Dad!

Sakina Fazal (15)
St Constantine's International School, Tanzania

StrEnGth of A FathEr

The only thing that keeps
you strong is your love

You are a father
that any daughter can trust

Through your love and strength
you have made all my dreams come true

My goal is to make you
the happiest father in the whole world

May God and all the angels
keep your strength of love the same forever.

Happy Father's Day!

Sabiha Fazal (12)
St Constantine's International School, Tanzania

DEar Dad

Dad, Dad, Dad
You make me feel as happy as a king
You are the best
You get a lot of trouble, but you manage to keep us happy
You make sure I get a good education
You get trouble to get my school fees
But never tell me about it or never let me feel it
Life without you would be impossible
You provide me with what I need
Dad, you are the best
I wish every child had a dad like you.

Bhavesh Chundawadra (14)
St Constantine's International School, Tanzania

A POEM For Dad

Dad, Dad, when you are good
You are very, very good,
Whenever I see you
I feel like I have got happiness.

Dad, Dad, without you I cannot live,
Dad, you are everything to me,
Dad, without you there is no life.

Dad, I won't stay alive without you,
Dad, if you are not there I will be alone,
Dad, you are very, very good.

Ajmal Andani (15)
St Constantine's International School, Tanzania

untitled

Dad, you gave me life,
Dad, the best in the world,
Dad, you are my god,
Dad, you are my life
   which God gave you.

Dad, my angel of life,
Dad, you are my blessing,
Dad, you are my love,
Dad, I believe in you,
   which God gave you.

Dad, I pray for you,
Dad, I worship you,
Dad, you are my life
   which God gave you.

Juzer Chomoco (14)
St Constantine's International School, Tanzania

Daddy's girl

When you were young, pony-tailed,
Face full of freckles,
Were you a daddy's girl?
I was, I still am.

Did you look to him for your security,
For love and attention,
For the understanding
And the patience you lacked as a child?

My daddy was the centre of the small world,
The focus of my attention,
The star that lit my life, shining bright,
Shining still in my heart.

The years have led me here,
Whethered with maturity and responsibilites,
And I see more clearly now,
The hardship, burdens of love,
And the small sacrifices he made for me,
For our family.

He created stability, a place to call home,
All the photographs I browse through
Of a child long forgotten, scarecely remembered,
Smiling, so happy and so loved,
The mere thought of becoming that role model
Is enough to send me cowering, afraid ...
Looking for guidance.

Zamina Fazal (12)
St Constantine's International School, Tanzania

Daddy's Love

Daddy, without you my life would be incomplete,
You fulfil all my needs,
You give me whatever I ask for,
If it wasn't for you
I would never have been in this world,
I would never have gone to school,
I would never have food on the table,
I wouldn't have clothes on my body.
Since the day Mama gave birth to me
In that small little hospital room,
You gave so much to me,
And I thank you for all.
Daddy, I appreciate your love and dedication,
I don't know how to thank you,
But all I can say is that
I love you from the bottom of my heart,
And happy Father's Day.

Shoeapane Griffiths Matete (15)
St Constantine's International School, Tanzania

Dad!

I remember the day you told me
I was the perfect girl to be given to you,
How warm and special I felt,
That has always made me strong,
We have been through ups and downs,
But that is always meant to happen.

I thought you never loved me,
When you beat me,
Maybe those were your special ways I guess,
Sometimes when I lie to you,
I feel so quilty inside.

When others turn and walk away,
When I'm alone and I need someone to comfort me,
You are always there, you understand,
You go through so much for my sake,
You always wake up early to work,
For my well-being.

I promise I will keep your spirit forever with me,
I love you Dad, you are the greatest,
I promise I will never let you down.

Melba Jackson (15)
St Constantine's International School, Tanzania

My Super Dad

My dad has many tattoos
Like tigers, dragons and knives
Skeletons, bagpipes and names
Countries, flags and fire
My dad is great
I love him loads
He's the best and he's better than the rest
He picks me up when I am down
He's fast
He's strong
He's mean
He's great and I love him
He reads me books at night and I get a fright
My dad's smile shines like the sun
It blinds my mum
He flies like a plane
He acts to me like a chain.

My dad is a carpet fitter
He earns money
And he is funny
Sometimes he acts like a dummy
My dad likes booze
And he likes to snooze
He is a super dad
He likes adventures
He is Scottish
He used to live in a cottage.

My dad is wicked
He likes football
He is very, very tall.

Andrew Paul Cutler (9)
St Dominic's Primary School, Homerton

My Father's Day Poem

Roses are red, violets are blue,
Father's Day is going to be great,
I am making it special just for you.
You make me happy, you make me smile,
You make me have manners like it's in a file.
When I give you my present
You will keep it for a long while.
Is it true or is it fake?
I'll make it good for my father's sake.
You are good to me, I am good to you.
You are really good to me
On this day I will do everything for you.

If you lift a finger to try and call me
I'll come running upstairs and give you your tea.
Whatever you want I will try and get you it.
I will give you a hint, it is a piece of ...
You'll find out the rest,
You will think it's the best.
I hope you like your gift,
It took me a long time to find it.
When you have it I know you will cherish it.

You will also get a Father's Day bear,
It will be wonderful.
Imagine if it can cut your hair
You are very kind,
I hope you are enjoying there.
It will be really nice if you were back here.
You are my dad.
I know you won't be mad
And you are not a bad dad.
You are good like you should
And I will always be reading a book
And pretend that I am famous.

Happy Father's Day, hope you enjoy it.

Saabah Asiedu (9)
St Dominic's Primary School, Homerton

My Father

My father,
He is so kind,
He is generous,
He is helpful,
I will always love him,
I will always remember him,
My father.

Jithin Selvamon Selvaraj (10)
St Dominic's Primary School, Homerton

To My Loving Father For Father's Day

Dad, Dad
You're a great lad
You were there when I was born
Looking at my face when I was crying
When I hug you
I feel so great
You are a great man
Cooking eggs in the pan
I will always love you
In everything I do
You work hard
You never look sad
You are always confident
You are nice and pleasant
I would not let you go
You like to join the flow
I love you

God bless you, Dad.

Michael Ogunsola (11)
St Dominic's Primary School, Homerton

Father's Day!

On Father's Day this year,
I would be committing an awful crime,
If I didn't tell my dad I loved him,
Forever and all the time!
I can always go and talk to my dad,
Whenever I'm sad or down,
With his loving personality,
He can wipe away my frown.
We've shared many laughs,
And together had a good cry,
But in the end he's still my dad,
And I'll love him till I die!

Leonita Gaspard (11)
St Dominic's Primary School, Homerton

HE IS ...

A man with respect
As jolly as the sun
Muscular like a boxer
Likes to play a game of footie with me
A game of golf on a Sunday morning
Extremely hilarious
As cuddly as a bear
A man who likes a party
Admired by many
Always dusting around
A man who loves his family.

Emma Woonton (10)
St Dominic's Primary School, Homerton

HE is ...

A tall, strong man
Extremely handsome
Good at everything in the world
A hard-working man
A very good painter
But he gets paint all over himself
Loved by everyone
A gentleman
The best at everything
Always great
My best mate.

Liam O'Neill (9)
St Dominic's Primary School, Homerton

My ultimate Dad

My dad is the best in the west.
He is thirty-five.
It's a good thing that I'm alive.
Dad, oh Dad, I'm not being silly.
Dad, oh Dad, always watching TV.
Daddy gave me a PS2.
Daddy really loves me, *yahoo!*
My dad is always there for me.
My dad always makes me say please.
My dad is the ultimate dad.

My dad is strong.
He doesn't get much wrong.
He is kind and gives me things.
He gave my mum a super ring.
My dad was a cook.
He cooks from a great big book.
Now his job is a mystery.
My dad took me on a ferry.
His birthday is September the twenty-third.
My dad really likes birds.

My dad helps me with tests.
My dad never really rests.
He stays up till 6am in the morning.
He always goes to sleep snoring.
Sometimes he is boring.
My dad likes eating anything.
My dad really hates to sing.
My dad is blazing like fire.
My dad is good at wires.
My dad is the ultimate dad.

Jack Alexander Yusuf (8)
St Dominic's Primary School, Homerton

HE is ...

Always car buying
A DIY expert
Admired by all who know him
Sometimes drunk at Christmas
Always great, my best mate
As fat as a cuddly bear
As ginger as the sun
A man who turns from white to black
A gentleman, a joker, a madman
Always drinking Coca-Cola.

Kai Parkinson (10)
St Dominic's Primary School, Homerton

HE ...

Is a gentleman
Drives a great car
Is always at work
Is as cuddly as a bear
Is always there for me
Smells really nice
Is a great worker
Snores which always wakes me up - *zzzzzzzzz!*
Likes music but he doesn't play it loud
Is my best friend
Buys me stuff
And I love him.

Junisa Sheriff (10)
St Dominic's Primary School, Homerton

mY FathEr is ...

A fearsome, funny person
Adored by everyone he knows
There through thick and thin
Always there for me
A giver of hundreds of hugs throughout the years
A person who enjoys DIY, *boom, crash, bang!*
Ready to help me in all my needs.

My love for you will never end.

Gloria Odumosa (9)
St Dominic's Primary School, Homerton

Dads Are The greatest!

With his short, sparse, brown hair,
He doesn't like to be called Sir.
My dad has always been there for me,
He always has a cup of tea.

People think their dads are mad,
Sometimes I think mine's as bad.
But when you see cowboys jumping around,
I know not to speak and say a sound.

Out at eight in the morning,
Goes to work as day is dawning.
He's out all day painting,
Now it's time to rest and sit waiting.

Hard-working and good fun,
Whenever he's finished he has a bun.
Love your dad as much as you can,
And always try to be his number one fan.

Rachel Dickson (12)
St Malachy's High School, Castlewellan

Dad Rocks!

295

MY DAd SEaMUS

Up at 7, too early for me.
I don't see him till we sit down at tea.
Out to the farm he then does go
And in at 8 for his weekly show.
Clint Eastwood and John Wayne,
It seems like the same show repeated over again.
He sits on his chair with his feet on the hearth,
It's where he belongs, special in our hearts.

Roisin Malone (12)
St Malachy's High School, Castlewellan

MY FATHER'S DAY POEM

F ootball's one of his hobbies
A lways jokes with me
T akes me to football on Sundays
H ates seeing Man United win
E njoys watching Gaelic football
R eally likes playing golf
S unday dinner is his favourite

D rives a grey Renault Scenic
A lso likes eating salads
Y oung at heart is what he is.

Darren Burns (12)
St Malachy's High School, Castlewellan

My Dad

My daddy is called Brendan,
He is a lovely man.
He does his very best for me,
Everything he can.

My dad is tall and has brown hair,
He has brown eyes too.
When I have my problems,
He's the one I tell.

He likes to drive a nice, big car,
To take him to work and back.
He likes to drive a nice, bright car,
Never brown or black.

My dad is a mechanic,
He works on vans and cars.
He sometimes works on lorries,
He works for hours and hours.

He lets me go to funfairs,
He lets me go to the pool.
He lets me off with lots of things,
He really isn't cruel.

Happy Father's Day.

Christopher McClean (12)
St Malachy's High School, Castlewellan

My Dad

My dad
Gets very mad
When I do something wrong
Or when my sister sings a song

My dad is very funny
And always gives me lots of money
He does not like watching football
And he is not very tall

He likes to go on his motorbike
With his friends to France
He always likes to play the guitar
And he always washes the car

He is a great fisherman
And he's always driving a yellow van
He goes hunting when he gets a chance
And never, ever likes to dance.

Matthew Harrison (12)
St Malachy's High School, Castlewellan

My Dad

My dad is called Dom, he is very funny.
He hates it when it's too warm or too sunny.
He loves us all and we all love him back.
His hair is grey and it used to be black.
He shouts sometimes but calms down in the end.
I think it's because we drive him round the bend.
You're probably wondering what I'm trying to say,
It's fairly simple:

Happy Father's Day.

Aidan McGahan (12)
St Malachy's High School, Castlewellan

A POEM TO MY Dad

My dad is called Michael and he has brown hair.
He is medium height with sparkling, green eyes.
He always wears jeans with a jumper to match
And that's what makes him my dad.

My dad works as a joiner and likes it a lot.
He cuts, he saws, he mends and he sticks.
He goes to work early and comes home late
And that's what makes him my dad.

My dad is quiet and doesn't shout a lot.
He likes to help with homework and does it quite a bit.
He always tries to make me laugh when I'm feeling down
And that's what makes him my dad.

My dad always finds something to do.
He loves gardening, cleaning and washing the car too.
He takes me to places I have never been before
And that's what makes him my dad.

Rosemary O'Loughlin (12)
St Malachy's High School, Castlewellan

My Dad

My dad is a nice lad
Who never acts really bad.
He's got a black beard
And he's never feared
Because all of us love him.

He's got light blue eyes
And he makes us lovely Sunday fries.
He plays football in the back garden
And is always polite when he says pardon.
He's the best dad I think.

His birthday is in September
And we always remember.
Mum and Dad have been married 25 years
And he likes having a few beers
And we love him for who he is.

He likes watching football on the television
I think he likes Arsenal same as me
That's the right decision!
So we've got one thing to say,
Happy Father's Day.

Conor Boden (12)
St Malachy's High School, Castlewellan

My Dad! He's The Best

My dad is so great,
He never lets me out on a date,
He is so much fun,
He can lift a ton,
And I love him!

He makes the nicest dinners,
He always calls us winners,
He's the best,
The best there can be,
Because he loves me!

He likes to play basketball,
He's more than six foot tall,
He's a giant in my eyes,
And makes us lovely pies.
That's my dad and I love him!

He is so big,
He is so strong,
And I like to tag along,
We shoot baskets together,
In all kinds of weather.
That's my dad and I love him.

Rebecca McGreevy (12)
St Malachy's High School, Castlewellan

Father's Day Poem

F ighting with me while the dinner's burnt.
A mad one after I beat him at golf.
T aking me to golf on Sundays.
H earing him pull up when he gets back from England.
E ating so fast to go and watch golf.
R oaring when a rat comes.
S inging along when a song comes on.

D rawing funny faces on the window.
A golfer he is; a golfer he will be.
Y es, he is a dad but to me he is the best.

Kieran Cleversley (12)
St Malachy's High School, Castlewellan

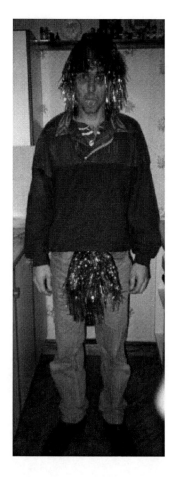

Dad

F athers are great like mine
A nd you'll know in my rhyme
T he things he does with me
H oping to play footy, *yippee!*
E venings he's tired
R eally he's usually wired
S houts when Liverpool lose

D efinitely loves a snooze
A lthough I like him a lot
Y ou'll really like him too.

Gerard Corrigan (11)
St Malachy's High School, Castlewellan

mY Dad!

P rancing around
O r teasing me
E ven annoying my mum
M essy and mischievous habits, his
S inging is what I really hate!

F orever biting his fingernails
O r playing trains with my brother
R umbling and tumbling and mucking around

D aft and crazy as well
A ll of these things describe my ...
D ad!

Madeleine Pegrum (12)
The Cotswold School, Cheltenham

Dad!

F unny, fabulous, faithful, fair.
A ctive, adamant, able, there.
T actful, talented, technical, tough,
H appy, handy, hopeful, rough.
E nergetic, engaged, embarrassed, even.
R obust, right, ravenous, clean.
S omething special and complete he is.

D aring, careful but sometimes in a tizz.
A ble to do almost anything.
Y et not as good as next-door's king.

F actual in his business,
O r fictional in his fitness.
R eally clever on 'Millionaire'.

A lways answers correct, so there.

S o where does he get this special way
P ersonal way, to save the day?
E ffective is he.
C apable for me.
I nto mowing,
A nd hedge trimming.
L azy, loopy, sometimes droopy.

D evil and snoopy.
A lovely dad he is
D oing what he does for *me!*

Zoë Willis (12)
The Cotswold School, Cheltenham

My Dad

My dad's always there,
Always there for me.
He always makes the world
Seem much better for me.

He's always doing things,
Special things for me.
He's always giving up his time
To spend it with me.

The last time he was seen,
He was doing something for me.
He probably is the best,
He definitely is for me.

Jack Howarth (12)
The Cotswold School, Cheltenham

Dad, i LOVE you

You're the dad who makes me laugh,
When I'm sad you make me smile,
You say goodnight with a big tickle hug,
You're special and I love you, Dad!

You help me with my school homework,
Especially with my science,
For you are the *best* science teacher,
You're special and I love you, Dad!

I'm sorry when I get in strops with you,
It's just me growing up, I guess,
I love you really even when you annoy me,
You're special and I love you, Dad!

Some people are embarrassed by their dads,
I know I am sometimes,
But you rock and are cool in my heart!
You're special and I love you, Dad!

Philippa Lane (11)
The Cotswold School, Cheltenham

Father's Day

Every year there is one special day
Only for dads
Who have always been there for you
And who is glad to be your dad
No matter what you do they are always caring
Who help you out
And always have a place in their heart for you.

Your dad knows what you're thinking
They always listen to you
And try to protect you no matter what you do
And is like one of your best friends.

If things go wrong
Your dad tries to pull it back together
Plus your dad's love plays a part in your life
Most of all he loves you and wants you to do good
So happy Father's Day, Dad
I'll always remember you.

Roy Hackett (11)
Thorpedene Junior School, Shoeburyness

My Dad

My dad is the best in the world,
He cooks, he cleans,
He eats all his beans
And that's why I love my daddy.

My dad is the best in the world,
He makes me laugh all the time
And that's why I wrote this rhyme.
That's why I love my daddy.

Kerry McCrory (8)
Thorpedene Junior School, Shoeburyness

MY Dad

M y dad is the best in the world,
Y ou would love him to be yours.

D oes all the driving and makes the tea,
A nd plays games with me,
D eserves a gold medal,
D elighted that he's my dad,
Y ou are the best dad in the world!

Sian McCrory (11)
Thorpedene Junior School, Shoeburyness

MY DADDY

M y dad is the best
Y ou would love him like I do

D ad is great, he cooks and cleans
A nd he loves me very much! He ...
D eserves nothing better than the best.

Amber Johnson (11)
Thorpedene Junior School, Shoeburyness

information

We hope you have enjoyed reading this book - and that you
will continue to enjoy it in the coming years. If you like
reading and writing poems and stories drop us a line, or give
us a call, and we'll send you a free information pack.

**Write to
Young Writers, Remus House, Coltsfoot Drive,
Woodston, Peterborough PE2 9JX
(01733) 890066**

**Alternatively check out our website:
www.youngwriters.co.uk**